This book will be a blessing to each one who reads it. The heart of the work is to build up and encourage. How refreshing to hear from someone who has seen the best and the worst of "the church", who is still in the church, still believes in the church, and explains why. I heartily recommend *Exits* to you.

Pastor Brent Cantelon.
Sr. Pastor, Christian Life Assembly (CLA)

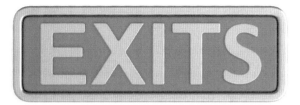

EXITS

Should I Go ?

Should I Stay ?

Grant Holcombe

Railroad Pictures from the private collection of Jack Porzig Surrey, B.C.
Vineyard picture provided by Domaine de Chaberton Estate Winery.
Additional photographs purchased from Shutterstock.

Printed in Canada

ISBN: 978-1-4866-0150-9

Word Alive Press
131 Cordite Road, Winnipeg, MB R3W 1S1
www.wordalivepress.ca

WORD ALIVE PRESS
Just Write!

MIX
Paper from responsible sources
FSC® C016245
FSC www.fsc.org

Cataloguing in Publication may be obtained through Library and Archives Canada.

DEDICATION

This book is dedicated to my parents James and June Holcombe and my wife's parents Robert and Ruth Low. Their lives are a testimony that contributed greatly to who Cherril and I have become. Their legacy has passed on to our children and grand children and is of great worth.

> 6 *Train up a child in the way he should go, And when he is old he will not depart from it.* (Proverbs 22:6, NKJV)

ACKNOWLEDGEMENTS

THANKS TO MY PIT CREW.

My test listener and sounding board. She claims to have "heard" every word numerous times! So much so that she feels she can quote the book by memory. My wife.

Cherril Holcombe

My Test Readers and good friends:

Grant Bateman

Pastor Brent Cantelon

My Christian editor:

Ed Strauss

Web and Media consultant and designer.

Jonathan Culley

Dale Huberts – A good friend and talented artist. Thank you for your assistance in helping me make decisions while working with the cover designers.

EXITS

CONTENTS

ENTRANCE: PREFACE

An image has formed in my mind, accompanied by a very strong thought that has been on my heart for a number of years. I've been struggling with, praying over, and thinking about this image ever since. It won't seem to leave me. I had the desire to write this after reading another one of those books explaining how the Christian Church "needs to tear up what we have and get back to the basics." But what exactly does "getting back to basics" mean? The book I read didn't seem to have the answer. It for sure detailed the problems. Not exactly a new approach. Tear the Church up? But for what purpose? In fact there must be hundreds of books on the shelves that are based upon this topic.

So why this book, and how will it be different? Will this book even be of interest to readers? You will need to read it and then let me know. I pray that the same questions that require an answer are on your heart as well. Besides, I think my wife may feel some relief, because if I get all this down on paper, I won't feel the need to burden her with my musings.

Over the years I have seen the Church go through various transitions as the new and improved models emerge. If you have been a Christian for any length of time you know what I am talking about. In some ways it is like watching the new model cars being rolled out each year. What will this year's model look like for the New or Emerging Church?

I wish to write this book from a positive perspective. I don't wish to break down or destroy what I feel God has already set up as His Church. The object of my search is not to find something new and improved, but to try and define what the original design and purpose of the Christian Church is, and how that applies today.

Another book that simply details the problems and errors of a particular system isn't of any value. Merely creating doubts in the reader's mind has no potential for finding answers or creating unity. Such a book can only be destructive. It is simple to detail questions but it is more profitable to assist fellow Christians in discovering a productive solution to the questions created. Suggesting that we need to be in a different era or have some new model is no help as we can only live in the here and now. Moving back in time 2,000 years is not an option. Moving to another community is possible but may not be practical. God put us in this time and place for a reason.

The Church has been given an operator's manual detailing how Christians can live in harmony and be in a relationship with Jesus. Rewriting the manual to fit our personal point of view isn't an option. A new system of Church or a new form of worship will not bring people to the saving knowledge of Jesus. Without the presence of Jesus, the members of any Church are part of nothing more than another service club.

Any group of believers should be able to work together in productive harmony regardless of their time period, their geographical location, their denomination or their community—whether poor or prosperous. The deep and weighty doctrines will be left to others more scholarly than me. The Church was not intended to be so complex when God set up his original design, but because we are human, we feel the need to make it complicated. If it was simple then we wouldn't have a need for some of those brilliant people profiting from bringing out new models for the Church each year. Oops! This is to be remain a positive book, Grant!

EXIT 1

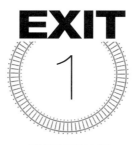

EXIT SIGNS

As I mentioned, I have an image in my mind that has been troubling me for a number of years. I don't like to call it a vision, but in this day of Digital, I think the term "image" will be sufficient.

I see a building that bears similarity to a church building but it has been modernized to not have any features that might distinguish it as a Christian church. Out front is a sign board advertising the many programs being offered that might appeal to the passers-by, Christian or non-Christian.

I slow down for a closer look and I notice that people are walking around the building, looking into windows. They are finding it difficult to locate an access door. They can only stand outside the building and look in, wondering what is going on inside. Intrigued by this, I walk up and talk to a few of the people who are looking in the windows and ask what this is all about.

They reply that they are Christians but have not attended Church for a number of years. Various reasons are given, but a common comment is that they at one time attended, but for various reasons decided it was no longer "satisfying their need to worship God." A common comment is that "they are all churched out."

Some of these people say that they haven't been in Church for many years, not since attending Sunday school as a child with their parents. Others state that they once came to the Church for some special meetings, asked Jesus into their hearts, but after a couple of years they felt lonely and empty and just sort of drifted away. They all state that they still believe in Jesus and still know that they remain Christians, but they just grew tired of the empty and disappointed feeling they experienced each time they attended Church.

This feeling of emptiness and disappointment each time they attended only seemed to grow in intensity. In fact, some used to drive by the church each day on their way to work, but just the sight of the building added to their feeling of anxiety and stress, so they deliberately changed their drive so they wouldn't be reminded of this feeling of anxiety.

I was drawn to the commonality of the people's comments and joined them to have a look in the windows. Once I looked in from the point of view of an outsider, I started to experience some of the feelings that they were describing. I confided to a couple of people standing close by that I sometimes attend this Church as well, but I had not been attending all that regularly. "I have a very busy schedule. My wife likes to travel and wants to take a few trips. We still call this our Church home, but we are not that involved any longer."

I offered to assist a couple of people looking into the windows to see if together we could locate an entrance. "Let me help you," I said. "I think I may still remember where the door is." We took a couple of trips around the building. One of the people mentioned that this was one of the reasons that they stopped attending this Church—it was always so difficult to find the door of acceptance. They were told to feel welcome and told that they had a place, but in their hearts they just didn't seem to fit. Some of them told me, "Most times it seemed that the reason they wanted us to feel welcome was that they wanted or needed something from us."

After the third trip around the building we finally found a door. It was a very small door with a sign over it that said, "Welcome to the House of the Lord." After reading this sign we determined that this must in fact be a church building and this was the entrance. Once inside, we were greeted by a few enthusiastic people welcoming us with smiles, and giving us papers that advertised all of the many exciting programs that their Church was offering this week. We were assured that we would not want to miss any of these, that we needed to come back and take them in. I now started to understand the feelings my two guests described when they used to attend. Even though I had been attending for a number of years, the Happy People shaking my hands didn't know who I was either.

There appeared to be some sort of meeting going on. Things were done well! Everything was very professional. The quality and the timing were precise. My first thought was that this is as good as any show you could buy a ticket for. The music was awesome, and the graphic presentations were high quality, showing all of the many great things that this particular organization accomplished. Many exciting things seemed to be coming up, and we were once again assured that we would not want to miss out. The speaking was excellent and very polished and well-presented, and the mood was meant to be uplifting. Full marks on all points.

Something appeared to be missing, however, and those old feelings were recalled and started to well up within us all. One new friend, the man whom I was standing beside, leaned over and asked me, "Is it always like this?" I thought that he was impressed by the activities, energy, and enthusiasm, but wasn't sure, so asked him to explain his question.

He replied, "The energy level appears to be good, but in looking at the faces of those standing around me, I see the same empty expressions and lack of enthusiasm that I once felt. People appear to be enjoying the performance and are raising their hands on cue, but look sort of detached. In looking around, I also see that a lot of seats are vacant—yet both the speaker and this bulletin are telling us that this is an organization that is truly filling a need."

I was struck by his comments. Upon careful consideration, I was compelled to agree.

Another observation that was even more difficult to explain was that there appeared to be a lot of exits leaving the building and identified as "Exit Only." After finding it so difficult to get into the building, I found it odd that the designer of the building would make it so easy to exit the building. What seemed even odder was the fact that even though the meeting was still going on, there were many people standing in the Exits. Many of the people had sort of blank, bewildered expressions on their faces as if they were trying to decide if they should stay a little longer, or just make an efficient and quiet exit when a break in the activity permitted. On a more careful examination, I noticed that a number of them seemed to be a bit further along in their decisions and, in fact, had their hands on the door handle and were prepared to Exit at that very second.

I said to the man standing beside me, "I appreciate you being so honest, and asking me your question a few minutes ago." I assured him that his question was a valid one and that it deserved an answer. Unfortunately, I did not have an answer for him. I then invited him to assist me to find an answer to his question. He agreed, adding that this question had been on his mind for a few years now.

I pointed to a couple of people who were already standing in one of the "Exit Only" doors. I said, "Let's speak to a few of the people that have already exited the building, and see if we can find out why they have made their choice to leave."

Once we were outside the building, and the Exit door closed behind us, my heart dropped. The number of people who were standing just outside the Exits was greater than the group of people who had recently found the small entrance and had entered. They all seemed to have the same expression of disappointment and bewilderment. They were not obviously settled in their decision to Exit, but they were leaving just the same. I felt an even greater despair when I turned around to see if I could reenter the building through the door that I had just walked out of. It did not have a handle on the outside! There was no way to return through it!

It was then that my eyes fell on the signboard outside the church. The topic of the sermon that morning was: "Fulfilling the Great Commission" I felt a keen pang of concern and disappointment.

Most of us are familiar with the digital photography available to us in many formats. We are even taking pictures (images) with our cell phones. Once you take an image, you can review it on the screen of your particular device, and then when you get home, download it to your computer and view it in higher resolution and in greater size. Once you look at the larger size you then see many other features that you didn't see on the original small screen. You then move the image to some editing software and prepare it for a print or a slide. Sometimes, in the process, you see features in the HD image that you didn't even notice while you were standing there taking the picture.

This is what I am referring to as the image in my mind. I am now downloading this image from my mind to my PC (Sorry, Mac people), editing it, and moving it to Power Point. My image is now in High Definition and ready for editing with Photo Shop. Now that I can see the finer details of the image, I think that "Exits" seems like a good title for this picture. I think the topic should go deeper—perhaps be a book. Yes. I have decided that this will be a book. The title will be "EXITS."

I am looking forward to reading what I am about to write. I love surprises but I hate unanswered questions. A good problem always deserves an answer; otherwise it is nothing more than negative dribble.

This image is now moved from my mind, converted to a word picture, and ready to be placed on a Power Point slide. It is amazing, however, what a slide or a quote taken out of context can be interpreted to mean.

If this question was posted on a slide, independent from the context of my image, what would you think?

Question: The man that I was standing beside leaned over and asked me, "Is it always like this?" I thought that he was impressed by the activities and enthusiasm taking place around him. I decided to ask him to explain his question.

If you think this is an image only of the Church I attend, then you are wrong. The Church is a collective term that Christ gave to the living, breathing souls who make up his body. Their collective presence together is the Church. Unfortunately, this image represents many Churches that I have become familiar with over the years.

This sounds like I have done a lot of Church-hopping. This is not the case! I have been a Christian for a lot of years, but through various contacts and connections I have been blessed to know a lot of good people in many good Churches. The fact is that I have only attended three Churches on a long-term basis. I was born into my first Church even before the word "media" was a word. Even more of a blessing, I have a lot of good friends and relatives who are pastors in various Churches around the country. The same underlying image seems to be present in an alarming number of Churches.

Fortunately, not all Churches are at the same place in the cycle at the same time. The Church appears to move in cycles of mountain tops and valleys and for some good reason not all Churches appear to be in the same cycle at the same time. This is why many Christians appear to be in an unsettled state and in constant motion as they drift from Church to Church.

I see a new facet of the image that I hadn't noticed at first. I change to a higher resolution for a closer look at what the image is showing. I now see that the Church represented is not a single Church but is, in fact, a composite made up of a number of Churches in a region. The people exiting are in a drifting process as they progress towards the Exits. Eventually, some make a final exit to a place of Church isolation.

In this illustration, the pastor and staff are supposedly part of the same body as the regular Church members, but in reality they are (to use an old expression), literally "poles apart." Polarization is taking place between two distinct bodies within the Church. Staff and laypeople do not appear to have a connection but are congregating like iron filings around the two ends of a magnet.

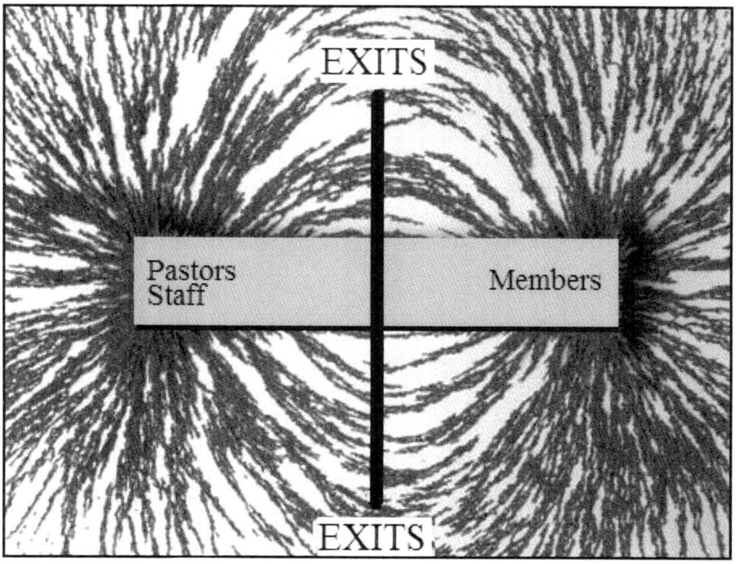

On one pole we see the Church pastors and leaders. We will identify them as the north pole. On the other pole we see the average laypeople attending Church. We will identify them as the south pole. Between the two poles is a neutral zone where those who are planning to leave gather.

The pastors and staff have become isolated while attempting to come up with new programs and activities to attract and keep laypeople gathered around the south pole. The need to keep the pole full is great, but their plans appear to have a lack of focus and consistency. The staff seems to lack understanding what the average family is looking for in their desire to worship. The laypeople, for their part, find that as they move towards the neutral zone it makes it easier for them to exit. As they exit they attract others to now move to the neutral zone. Perhaps the laypeople don't understand what Church is meant to be?

Of equal concern, we see pastors and staff at the north pole in a state of flux and drifting. Once again we see that as one leaves from the north pole to the neutral zone, other staff and pastors in turn become unsettled. Perhaps they also don't understand what Church is meant to be?

The drifters have developed a cleverly thought-out excuse for their drifting towards the Exit. Shift the blame to others to put a good spiritual spin on their own shortfalls. "We are not getting fed, and the teaching is so much better at XYZ Church." The other big excuse is the music. Music is a lightning rod, unfortunately, for the current Church movement and contributes to the cycles. "They have such a great music program at XYZ Church." This again shifts the responsibility from themselves and gives the appearance that they are well in tune with the current gospel music scene. Is this really what Church is all about—a great speaker or a great music program?

Would the Christian Church not be more productive if we could just settle down and do what God has for us, and worship the Lord? This is also a point of confusion. Do we really know what a Church should look like and do we really understand the meaning of worship? Let's see if we can find the answer. An answer is needed for both poles—north and south.

To emphasize my point: I had a good conversation with a pastor friend of mine a few years ago. To stop speculation, this friend is not from my Church so the innocent are protected. He is also not from my city, so even better. His concern is the fact that his Church is facing a challenge and showing poor growth, and as a result of poor growth the giving is down. With the giving down, a number of the programs are limited and, in fact, some of the staff may need to be let go. They had a retreat to study the current trends in Churches and had a consultant come up with the current strategy for Church growth. (Ever wonder who this "they" group is in a Church? All Churches have an undercover group known as the "they group," I think.)

They have been praying for direction and a solution to their current challenge. To back up this study, they sent out a few of the key "they" people in their Church to visit and observe other Churches around the country, in both Canada and the USA, that were demonstrating good growth.

It was finally determined that the solution was training and upgrading.

The senior pastor is a bit long in the tooth and his preaching style is a bit "old school." Plans are to enroll him in some public speaking courses, and assist him with a makeover of his pulpit presence. Further to this, the music program needs an upgrade. The quality of the music is "good," but it needs to be more in tune with the current trends and styles of music in the Christian music world. Key catch-phrases are bantered about: "The current trend in successful Churches is to use media as an *enhancement* to worship." "It is a known fact that a Church with a good pulpit presence and an up-to-date music program will demonstrate growth." To add the icing to the cake, the leadership of the Church has devoted time to prayer and fasting on this, and feels that, yes, this is what is needed to resume growth.

(Well. This should Git-R-Done. *My thought only.*)

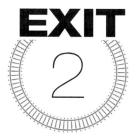

EXIT 2

AND THE TIDES EBB AND FLOW

Some drifting takes place over a number of years, and some takes place in about two-year cycles. My recent observations seem to indicate that Church drifts come in about two-year cycles. This drifting has some similarities to watching the tide ebb and flood. I live on the West Coast and spend considerable time boating off its coast. Look at a tide chart sometime and you will see the similarities to Church drift.

Now the boater side of me is starting to show. It is time to further your West Coast tide education. When the ocean recedes and empties a region, this is called the ebb tide. When the tide is between changes this is called slack tide. When the tide is coming in and refilling the empty places, this is called the flood tide. The tide does two complete cycles each day.

When you think about this ebb and flood in a Church body, it gives an unsettling indication that something underlying is not right. In a Church we look at a flood tide as good, and an ebb tide as bad. Something "happens" and then the ebb starts from one Church and the flood tends to gravitate to some other Church that is experiencing the mountaintop part of their cycle. This can be sparked by many things, but in most cases it appears to come down to four main points to those sitting in the pews. What are the four points that trigger the start of an ebb tide? Of course, it goes without saying that a lack of prayer and worship are key factors. This is the oxygen that is necessary to sustain spiritual life. Prayer and worship is the very reason God created man in the first place. But there are other deficiencies that will impede a Church. It would be nice if things were this simple. These four points do play a significant role in the changing tides. Miss these four points and you have a good possibility that the tide will begin to ebb:

Vision:

Every group or organization needs a vision defining its purpose and direction. A mission statement sometimes is used to define this purpose. Without a vision no focus is possible. What do you focus on if you don't have a vision? What is the core purpose for the Church? How can you be successful if you don't hang a target?

Frustration sets in. Without a vision, change is a constant, with little or no forward progress. The Church is just a group consistently moving towards the next great idea that the leader borrowed from some other successful Church.

Without a vision, the temptation is to chase after the visions of other Churches that are showing growth and blessings. Churches have personalities and attract Christians with similar passions. Failure comes when one personality type attempts to clone themselves from some other group that may or may not be a fit. Why did God place us together and whom do we serve? Every Church is unique in God's plan. Visualize what it is that God has for you and the Church that you have been planted in.

Direction:

This is the place for leadership to succeed or fail. Good leadership will help define the vision and assist the people to focus on the vision. The leaders must share the same vision and fully participate in it. The leaders must know and understand the people who are part of the Church. Who are these people and what is their passion and attributes? A Church is a living body and must be permitted to develop its own unique personality and build on its distinct attributes.

Visualize an Olympic athlete for a minute. The coaches play a huge role in assisting the athlete to win! Big Time! The coach must understand the athlete and share the athlete's vision and focus. The coach does not compete but helps the athlete to prepare to compete to his full potential. On this point, however: you do not take the coach of the men's wrestling team and have him coach the ladies' synchronized swimming team. The direction of the leaders must be compatible with the vision of the group. All must be on the same field.

Focus:

My son has a Golden Retriever that has a passion to retrieve. Her name is Lola. Put a ball in front of her and you have an excellent example of focus. If you don't have a ball handy she will find you a stick. She will sit motionless and just stare at that ball until you get the message that perhaps you should throw the ball for her. You cannot get her to stop staring at the ball until you throw it. She couldn't speak louder even if she could talk. Everyone knows what she wants and can't help but throw the ball.

Nothing will succeed without focus. Watch the Olympics and you will see absolute focus in a world-class athlete. The athlete focuses intently on the event that he intends to win. Prior to executing his particular event he pictures every move in his mind. He is mentally isolated from his surroundings. The crowd is going crazy, but he can't hear them. All he can see is the goal that he must achieve. He has the vision of winning and can do nothing but focus on that goal [vision]. How many Churches demonstrate this? Why do so many Churches then struggle? The answer is clear. They are not able to maintain their focus on their God-given purpose.

Consistency:

To express this another way, it is the ability to stay consistent. (Deep, eh?) Look at any successful person, organization, business, or church and you will see this characteristic big time! This is a major reason that some organizations are successful and others are not. From businesses to families, consistency is key. The successful ones are consistent and can stay on task for the long run. Those who fail generally are in a constant state of flux and always in startup mode, and rarely in growth mode. The phrase comes to mind, "They are given to change like the wind." Stay on track. Maintain an undivided and single focus. This is no different for a Church. I will talk more about this in Chapter 12 and throughout the book. Once a Church has found what it is good at (its calling) and whom they are to serve, they are to be consistent to this calling. Hold true to your core purpose and passion. In many Churches it seems like a constant procession of programs, staff and volunteer changes, and new and improved ideas. A fitting scripture is, "*he is a double-minded man, unstable in all his ways*" (James 1:8 NKJV). No wonder some Churches and people have challenges—always running like a lost man in the woods, but never moving forward. Running in circles is an image that comes to mind. Don't let this be your Church. Be consistent to who you are.

To be consistently starting over, or consistently running in circles does not define the true meaning of "consistency." This form of activity would be better described as failing. No matter what your chosen activity is—from church to family to business—take a pause and look back. Have you advanced to a better place in the last five years, the last ten years, the last few weeks even? If not, then lack of consistency will be at the top of the problem list.

Another cycle that I have noted over the years as the tide ebbs and floods for a particular Church body, is that this cycle seems to roll around about every 10 to 15 years. If this cycle doesn't take place, then in many instances the particular Church just ceases to be. A number of things can prompt the cycle and the outcome depends on how the leaders of the Church choose to react to the cycle. This is the best of the cycles I have seen, and I trust and pray that this cycle—in part—will once again be the case. You will see in a few moments why I make the comment "in part."

The Holy Spirit, in answer to prayer, chooses to revisit a Church or a geographic region that is in a period of spiritual drought. At some point during the ebb tide, a few good praying souls are ready to accept the Holy Spirit and allow him to take charge and build the Church once again. Read up on the great revivals down through history and you will see a common thread. Some call it Revival. Call it what you wish, the term is not important, but the effect is life-giving and transforming and will turn the tide from slack to flood.

The Church, out of desperation, gets back to basics. Simple stuff, really. All the programs have lost their appeal. The attendance is dwindling. The finances are declining. Exuberant teaching on "Giving Is Scriptural" is increasing. Nothing seems to be working. Some of the leaders and influential people of the Church leave. In some instances a group will attempt a Church split. Some of these actually leave quietly. The expression, "They are voting with their feet," comes to mind. This is not a good thing, however, as a number of good people get damaged in the process. Some may never return to Church. Things are desperate.

The leaders have nothing more to offer, so they fall back on praying and calling out to God for the Holy Spirit to once again take charge.

We see the waters start to stir. My best analogy, as you have now seen, is that this is the turning of the tide. Next time you are by the sea, try to spend some time and watch as the tide turns and the flood tide starts. It is very subtle and gentle at first and then it builds, until the full flood takes place with tremendous power and nothing can hold it back.

Energy starts to become evident in the Church, and people's spirits are lifted. The urge to attend Church once again returns, and they don't want to miss a meeting. The feeling is that if they are away then they will miss out on something. A sense of urgency prevails. The non-saved see that something is taking place in their friends' lives. Christians gain boldness to share the gospel with their friends and they see Church growth. Yes, drifters will come from other Churches, drawn by the excitement, but the real growth comes because the Church is growing with new Christians and not with transplants from other Churches. The bonus is the return of Christians who have been away for a long time. The Church is now seeing a move of the Holy Spirit.

Freedom and a spirit of generosity returns. The finances of the Church that were once a problem now show a surplus. The prosperity of the people starts to increase as they depend more on the Holy Spirit than prospering out of a legalistic approach to giving. Even though very little is now taught on giving, the giving increases. People give from their heart rather than giving because they have been told and pressured "that the Bible says to give."

Caution! This part offers some real challenges, however. Once the generosity kicks in and the offerings increase, some in the place feel that they should be beneficiaries of this newfound prosperity. **CAUTION with Flashing Red Lights!** With this influx of new cash, new programs increase. Some are good, but be careful about becoming dependant on "New Programs" or the Holy Spirit will leave again.

This is now the pivotal point.

I think this is often where the Church misses what is happening, and this causes the start of the next ebb tide. Look at the great Revivals. From start to finish, they usually last around five years, tops. What happens? Be vigilant and don't allow this to happen again if your Church is blessed by the Holy Spirit with a new opportunity.

But far too often the pendulum swings and the ego of man enters the picture! Someone wants to be king and claim ownership for the revival. Visitors from other areas come to observe the revival and want to take it back to their areas and Churches. Other visitors, "prophets and teachers," from faraway lands come to give teaching on revival and Church growth. We never heard of these guys until the action started. Some may have good intentions, but this is the time to have good people in the *home* Church as advisors who demonstrate the gift of discernment. Who better for a watch dog than a dog that the Church has raised from a pup—and who was praying for revival to come in the first place? Unfortunately these local gifts are often not consulted until it is too late, and the damage is done.

Others with flattering tongues come and influence the Church—the leaders and the "they group"—to think that *they* are the start and source of the coming nationwide revival. They now convince the Church that they will see the revival spread outside of their tent, and spread across the land with their particular Church as the epicenter. Does *this* ever get the juices going! And quite incidentally, these guys from distant cities have a great opportunity to clean up and leave with some great offerings—also known as cash or love offerings! Also, we acquire a few more kings in the process. Yes, we know that we are to be cautious of a flattering tongue, but it sure does feel good to have that old ego stroked.

With all of the activity, stroking, and ego-building, the need comes to expand to take care of this huge growth.

A building program is in order. With us being at the very hub of the coming revival, we need to have a World Evangelization headquarter. Check on some of the titles or names of these various Churches (and former Churches). Do you have any idea how many sets of blueprints have been produced for church building dreams that never got off the ground?

Here's a true story which serves as a good example. When I was in my early twenties I was an intern of sorts with a Church. This above scenario was playing out. I think the Church grew to about 500 people and the Church adopted a name-change and became called – THE WORLD CHRISTIAN CENTER! It isn't there any longer even though the future of the planet hinged on its very existence. Sure sounded huge, however, when all the commotion was going on. I refer back to some of my experiences from these days in the last chapter.

In some cases, the fallout is even greater and more tragic. With rock star status of some of the kings, it is easy for moral failure and the inappropriate use of the finances to take place. These are two biggies that old Satan loves to use—cash and out-of-control women/men. An explosive mixture!

A word to the wise is sufficient, hopefully. We pray that the Church doesn't make the same mistake twice, but actually, the number is greater than twice—a real tragic statement—perhaps hundreds or perhaps thousands of times. We mortals appear to be very slow learners.

You may think that this is an account of more recent times. You don't need to look that deep into Church history to see this drama played out time and time again. You may recall a book in the New Testament called the Acts of the Apostles.

As I understand it, the decline or downward transformation of the New Testament Church started within 100 years after the death and resurrection of Christ. Check the history of Christianity for a glimpse into the troubled past of the Church. Once the steadying hand of the Holy Spirit is weakened it doesn't take long. Once the old watch dogs known as the apostles and prophets died, things went into decline.

You may say, "These days, this scenario only takes place in Pentecostal Churches." Not so. Read on and study more. You will find a similar drama played out in any denomination. Perhaps you are familiar with the term "Church Split"?

Many reading this book may be "Protestants." And if so? A statement that many will find hard to swallow is the gratitude that we should express to the Catholic faith for preserving the texts of the scriptures. Even with them being the custodians of the scriptures for hundreds of years, however, the Catholic faith also fell into a sad state of decline. Remember when I said that this can happen with any denomination? Soon, wars raged as the opponents of the scriptures attempted to stop God's Word from being translated into the common tongues, and attempted to quash true Christian faith in Jesus. Have you heard of the Reformation? Take a look.

Talk about Church cycles of highs and lows! Our current roots stem back to the Reformation and the Holy Spirit reviving the spirit of a German monk, Martin Luther (10 November 1483 – 18 February 1546). Luther was a German monk, a former Catholic priest, a professor of theology and a seminal figure of a reform movement in sixteenth-century Christianity, subsequently known as the Protestant Reformation.

He strongly disputed the claim that freedom from God's punishment for sin could be purchased with money. At the time, in order to complete a building program, the Church adopted a newfound plan of selling Indulgences. This practice raised money to build a cathedral in Rome and it also offered the purchaser of the indulgence a pardon from sin and the freedom to enter heaven. Sort of a genetically-modified interpretation of scripture.

Unfortunately, not many have much knowledge of Martin Luther, but check it out. A brief summary: Luther taught that salvation is not earned by good deeds but received only as a free gift of God's grace through faith in Jesus Christ as redeemer from sin. His theology challenged the authority of the Pope of the Roman Catholic Church by teaching that the Bible is the only source of divinely-revealed knowledge, and put forth the revelation that all baptized Christians were a holy priesthood. Luther further discovered in the Book of Romans that we cannot purchase our salvation by doling out cash for indulgences, but that we are saved by grace and not by works or money.

Now, that was a long time of spiritual drought before Martin Luther came. No wonder it was called the Dark Ages. Even the Church that had the scriptures, the custodian appointed by God, abused them, and went into decline for almost 1,500 years. Now if that isn't a deep cycle, I don't know what is. Let's trust that the next turning of the tide does not last 1,500 years. Could this happen again? It is up to us.

EXIT 3

THE BRIDEGROOM IS COMING!

I LOVE WEDDINGS! MY WIFE AND I ARE FORTUNATE TO HAVE TWO children, a son and a daughter, and both are now married to great partners. I also love parties and social gatherings. (Ask Cherril!) The most exciting parties and social gatherings I have ever attended have been three weddings—my own, when my wife and I got married, and when our son and then our daughter got married.

If you have ever been a parent and have put on a wedding for your kids, I am sure you can relate. We had the excitement of a son's wedding and a daughter's wedding. Let me tell you, if you haven't figured this out yet, Dad's role is different in each one. They both involve a lot of work, and one involves a lot of work and expense. Neither one is cheap, but they are worth every penny. Guess which one was more expensive for me? Not my own. My wife and I had sandwiches in the church basement for our reception, no band.

In our western culture, the role of the bride's father is different than in the Bible culture. In the eastern culture, the groom's family takes the lead, and in our culture the bride and the bride's family takes the lead. Both roles are exciting for a father, especially when his children are marrying a Christian and wish to have a God-honoring wedding. We were blessed to have this to be the case.

A daughter's wedding, however, takes a lot more planning. The planning starts around the time she is five. This then gives lots of opportunity for her and her mother to make sure that every detail is covered. The whole thing is planned well in advance; all she needs to do is fill in the blank that says, "Groom's name."

Then came the big idea: "Let's host the reception at dad and mom's home. This will be really a lot simpler. dad, Really. All you have to do is pitch a tent in the pasture and bring in a couple of barbeques." No big deal! She forgot to mention the bands, the wagons, 250 guests, etc. etc. This will be the subject of my next book, "Hosting a Wedding in Your Field."

I can't help thinking that Jesus also loved weddings. His first miracle was at a wedding. He turned water into grape juice—or was that wine? Still trying to get this straight. It was a Jewish wedding, so I am not sure if that made it a Christian wedding or not. Must have been grape juice, since the readers of this book will be mainly Christians.

Jesus has made many references to the Church being his bride, and he is coming back for his bride. I can only imagine what that wedding is going to be like. I would love to be alive when this wedding takes place. It will be far better than any tent in a field. Can you imagine the planning and the celebration that is taking place when God the Father is planning a wedding for his Son?

If this is to be so, then why does his Bride seem to be having such difficulty getting ready? And why does his Bride in many cases appear to be on life support? And what can his Bride, the Christians who form the Church, do to get ready and healthy?

An even better question: What can I (or you) personally do to get ready to meet the Bridegroom as his Bride? The Church, after all, is not an institution; it is a living body made up of individual

Christians who collectively are the fleshly body of the Church. I trust that you and I are part of this body.

Perhaps the two portions of scripture below will shed some light on these questions.

> [1] *"Then the kingdom of heaven shall be likened to ten virgins who took their lamps and went out to meet the bridegroom.* [2]*Now five of them were wise, and five were foolish.* [3]*Those who were foolish took their lamps and took no oil with them,* [4]*but the wise took oil in their vessels with their lamps.* [5]*But while the bridegroom was delayed, they all slumbered and slept.* [6]*"And at midnight a cry was heard: '**Behold, the bridegroom is coming**; go out to meet him!'* [7]*Then all those virgins arose and trimmed their lamps.* [8]*And the foolish said to the wise, 'Give us some of your oil, for our lamps are going out.'* [9]*But the wise answered, saying, 'No, lest there should not be enough for us and you; but go rather to those who sell, and buy for yourselves.'* [10]*And while they went to buy, the bridegroom came, and those who were ready went in with him to the wedding; and the door was shut"* (Matthew 25:1-10 NKJV).

To some degree, I feel that the Church currently is in rest mode. Christ appears to be delayed, and the Church is taking this time to slumber and sleep. Don't you think it is about time to at least get up and buy some oil for our lamps so that we are ready?

I am not a theologian, but a simple guy who thinks that scripture may actually mean what it says. We are not reading Shakespeare here. As my English teacher used to ask, "What do you think he was saying?" Many times I felt like saying, "If *he* didn't know then how should I know?"

In my career, I am used to reading contracts, and I love contracts—they actually say what the writer meant to say. They are carefully-crafted with very specific language and words to accurately detail what the message is meant to be. Sometimes lawyers intentionally try to obscure this fact, but in the end they mean what they say. Can scripture be any different? Sometimes theologians have the same motives as lawyers, to confound the wise. If simplicity is the key, then perhaps some of the challenges that the Church is facing are contained in the simple statement:

> [2]*"For I am jealous for you with godly jealousy. For I have betrothed you to one husband, that I may present you as a chaste virgin to Christ.* [3]*But I fear, lest somehow, as the serpent deceived Eve by his craftiness, so your minds may be corrupted from the simplicity that is in Christ.* [4]*For if he who comes preaches another Jesus whom we have not preached, or if you receive a different spirit which you have not received, or a different gospel which you have not accepted—you may well put up with it!"* (2 Corinthians 11:2-4 NKJV).

The above scripture is a description of what Jesus meant the Church to be, highlighted with a caution of what the Church could become. The term "a *different* gospel" sparks thoughts of some new and blatant heresy. After careful thought about this possibility, I think the trap may be baited with a more subtle delicacy. Does the term Genetically Modified come to mind? Think of a Genetically Modified "interpretation" of the scripture. Looks, smells, and tastes like—and is not even altered from—the original text. Every aspect of the gospel is the same with one exception: the interpretations, or the genetic part, have been modified. Even though the text states the "*simplicity*" that is in Christ, many interpretations of the gospel attempt to make it very difficult and confusing.

Our new Bride is having some challenges in deciding what to serve for dinner. With an abundance of books and media about the menu, the opportunity is great for serving poor-quality food. The next chapter will focus on this real possibility of genetically-modified spiritual food. This is not all the responsibility of the Church, however. It takes true care and discernment on the part of believers—pastors and laypersons equally—to decide what to feed on. This is important, because some popular doctrines *have* actually modified our spiritual food.

This is not to suggest a new conspiracy theory about the Illuminati. A superficial look at Church history over the last 2,000 years will reveal that she has gone through some significant cycles—some good, and some not so good.

As I stated in my opening comments, I want this to be a positive book and a book that may be used as an aid to reconstruct the foundations that we can then build upon. I don't want to come off with some negative tirade that tears things down, leaves lots of questions and doubts, and a sense of hopelessness. Our God is bigger than that, but sometimes we are not able to see that.

In my line of work, I have the privilege to work with a few pretty serious business and financial problems. Unfortunately, some of these problems have been of my own making, in my own business, and they have given me the opportunity to pass on these hard-knock experiences to my clients.

One thing I have learned is that change begins with one person at a time. Problems and challenges of business, finances or families, are made up of collective problems of individuals. Once a problem has been identified then it is up to the individual to stay clear in the future. Unless the individuals change, the problem cannot be resolved. Is the problem with us, and in particular, is it with me?

Christians and the Church, in my opinion, are not any different. Unless I make some personal changes, then the Church cannot become the Bride that Jesus is waiting for. Will you assist me in making this change? I will attempt to make some changes, but you will also need to take a hard look at the areas that you need to change in your heart and life. Don't just read this collection of words without attempting to place yourself in the midst of them. The problem is not with the other guy, the Church, or with the music, it is with us. It is with me—the reflection in my mirror.

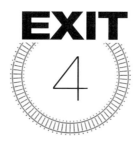

EXIT 4

WE ARE WHAT WE EAT

You have heard this comment many times: "You are what you eat." Any health book, weight loss program, and most parents interested in their kids' health, keep this fact in mind. Eat junk and you can expect to have some health and weight issues.

I am sure you have heard the term Genetically Engineered or Genetically Modified (GM). When something has been genetically engineered it appears to be the same as the natural product but some changes have been made to the genes—changes that are not easily detected. The commercial sale of GM foods commenced in 1994. Research the term "genetically modified" if you're not familiar with it. You'll find the topic fascinating—and perhaps a little unsettling.

GM foods look and taste like the original food, but genetically engineered plants are generated in a laboratory by altering their genetic makeup and are tested in the laboratory for desired qualities. This is usually done by adding one or more genes to a plant's genome using genetic engineering techniques. Once satisfactory plants are produced, sufficient seeds are mass-produced and sold to farmers. The farmers produce genetically modified crops, which also contain the inserted gene. The farmers then sell their crops as commodities into the food supply market.

Genetically modified plants are suspected of causing problems, however. I say *suspected*. According to some articles the problems appear to be unproved, but the symptoms are many. One symptom I am very aware of. One of my hobbies is beekeeping. You may have heard of a problem that has started to manifest itself in bee colonies in North America in about the last 10 years—Colony Collapse Disorder. It is suggested that with the production of GM crops there are new and serious problems with the honey bees. See what you think with this quote from an essay by Brit Amos Global Research, August 09, 2011:

"The genetic modification of the plant leads to the concurrent genetic modification of the flower pollen. When the flower pollen becomes genetically modified or sterile, the bees will potentially go malnourished and die of illness due to the lack of nutrients and the interruption of the digestive capacity of what they feed on through the summer and over the winter hibernation process."

The article goes on to describe diseases similar to colon cancer in humans. These are manifested in the bodies of the bees feeding on a GM crop. The article is linking part of the decline and failure of whole bee colonies to the ingesting of GM nectar and pollens. This is still unproven scientifically but the symptoms appear to be very real.

Ponder this statement for a moment before you move on. Just as with the beekeepers who are fighting to keep their colonies alive, can this be similar to what is going on undetected in our Churches. In short, what are we eating?

Seeds are now being genetically engineered that produce a crop that looks, smells, and tastes like the original but is significantly altered at the DNA level to produce only sterile seeds that will not germinate. Do you think this may be similar to what is described in 2 Corinthians 11:3 (NKJV)? *"But I fear, lest somehow, as the serpent deceived Eve by his craftiness, so your minds may be corrupted from the simplicity that is in Christ."* As far as Eve could tell, the forbidden fruit looked, tasted, and did nothing but good. To build on this thought, see what was going through Eve's mind as she was standing in the produce department, so to speak: *"So when the woman saw that the tree was good for food, that it was pleasant to the eyes, and a tree desirable to make one wise, she took of its fruit and ate"* (Genesis 3:6 NKJV). Looked good! Why not take some and eat it? She gave no thought to the notion that Satan had taken the Word of God and genetically modified it.

Most of us are familiar with Mark 4:24-32 which talks about the mustard seed, the little seed that grows into a large bush. We have heard all sorts of interpretations about what the bush signifies and what the significance of the birds sitting in the branches is. I will leave the interpretations to those smarter than me. A huge caution, however, is contained within this parable of Jesus:

> [24] *"Then He said to them, 'Take heed what you hear. With the same measure you use, it will be measured to you; and to you who hear, more will be given.* [25] *For whoever has, to him more will be given; but whoever does not have, even what he has will be taken away from him'"* (Mark 4:24-25 NKJV).

"Be careful what you hear." The words that we allow to enter our mind through our ears are small seeds that can grow into bushes that can influence us greatly. The influence we receive, however, may not always be positive or contribute to our spiritual health.

This is a wise caution presented to us by Jesus: *"Be careful what you hear."* So the obvious response is then, "How can I be careful?" This would imply that we need to have some form of filter that will help us to discern what we listen to or not. As a Christian we have the scripture as our filter, which in turn powers our spiritual senses to accept or reject something that we are hearing. The Word of God is like our spiritual immune system.

What we eat does affect our health. So can what we hear, what we read, and what we see or look at. They all impact us. What seeds do people plant in their minds, and how does this play into the sickness that is causing people to exit Church? Even more important is, once they leave Church they separate themselves from all of the support and teaching of being part of the body of Christ—and the weeds start to grow even faster.

We must take personal responsibility for ourselves and manage what we permit to enter our minds. We can control what seeds we are planting and we can take steps to pull the weeds that will cause us to grow weak and separate us from the body. I must control what I eat in order to maintain good health and growth. The same is with my walk with Jesus. A good healthy relationship with other Christians at Church is part of this healthy walk.

Another caution, however, should be considered, and that is a caution to those who teach. There are many voices in the Church that can influence the body. To those who teach—the pastors, for one—be careful what you are teaching. Make sure you know what you are talking about, and make sure that some interpretation of scripture is not laced with a personal motive or agenda. Both the speaker and the listener should have discernment to filter what they are feeding and eating. Both sides of this equation can play into the disease of exiting the Church.

Genetically modified food has caused quite a buzz on the health scene. Genetically modified food, looks, tastes, smells, and feels just like the parent food that started the process. Modify a tomato and both tomatoes look and taste the same. Only a Biochemist could tell the difference. The difference is something much more subtle than our senses can easily detect. The change is in the very DNA of the particular food. You can eat it and not even know you are eating a modified food. The jury is still out on whether or not it has any side effects to the consumer.

I would like to use an interesting discovery *that I think I made* this spring about Genetically Modified food. Read the story and then you make the decision. It is not scientific. It just is what I observed. Don't light your hair on fire as this is far from a scientific experiment. Just me and my bees.

Here it comes. Some have been asking if I will bring my bees into this book. I wasn't sure, but now it looks like this is the place. I am a beekeeper and look forward to a honey crop each year—nothing better than pure, unprocessed honey straight from the honeycomb. I always promote my honey with the statement that my honey has all of the goodness that the bee placed into it and nothing has been removed except the sting. Good commercial, hey? Want some?

This spring I was replacing some of the bees that had died over the winter and needed to feed them to give them a good start. I normally feed them in the spring with sugar syrup. I decided to try and go one better this year and feed them pure honey instead of sugar. Or I thought it was pure honey.

I was running low on my own natural honey, so I went to a retailer and bought some "cheap honey." The reason it was cheap honey is that it was canola honey. It looked similar to my natural honey, had the consistency of the natural honey, and had all of the properties of my natural honey. It even had "Pure Unprocessed Natural Honey" on the label. I must admit that it didn't taste as good as my natural honey. Well, my bees also figured out that it wasn't as good as the natural honey either.

I filled the feeders of each hive with this pure canola honey and placed them in the hives. I discovered that the bees were eating some of it, but not in the quantities that they should have been consuming for good health. What should have been consumed in about 10 days was still partially unconsumed after three weeks. They were eating only enough to survive, but not enough for the hive to thrive and produce new brood. Increasing the amount of brood in the hive is crucial for a good honey crop.

After three weeks I pulled out the half-full feeders and discovered that the canola honey had started to turn to a thickened mass and had almost a waxy consistency to it. It didn't look that great either. No wonder the bees were not eating it. The bees obviously had the "discernment" that something was not right about what I was feeding them. Discernment. Now that is a good Bible word. Perhaps we humans should learn to rely more on this.

I cleaned the feeders and removed all of the canola honey sludge. What a mess. I then added pure sugar syrup made from pure cane sugar. I added four liters of syrup per hive. The bees cleaned it all up in five days and were asking for more. Over the following week they consumed another four liters per hive, as well as some pollen, and the hive started to thrive and produced the brood that I was looking for.

Now that the blueberries have started to blossom and other wild flowers are present in the fields they are no longer eating the sugar syrup but much prefer the natural nectar from the local blossoms. The bees thrive much better once the natural blossoms start to appear and they can shift from processed food to the all-natural food.

This, of course, needed some investigation. Was something wrong with the canola honey? It is pure and people are eating it all the time. Why? Because it is pure, tastes sort of like good honey, and it is cheap. Ah, but why is it cheap? Originally, canola was bred naturally from rapeseed at the University of Manitoba, Canada in the early 1970s, but it has a very different nutritional profile. Genetically modified rapeseed oil may also be referred to as canola oil and is considered safe for human consumption. Now that is an encouraging statement. It is "considered" safe for human consumption.

Canola was developed because the parent rapeseed oil was produced in the 19th century as a source of a lubricant for steam engines. It was less useful as food for animals or humans because it has a bitter taste. By changing the DNA of the grain, science was able to make something that is different from the parent not-entirely-edible grain. We are now able to eat steam engine oil. Oh yum! Good stuff! At least you won't squeak.

Canola is a genetically modified grain that produces large amounts of oil, pollen, and nectar. I like the assurance that we are given with this. It is "considered safe for human consumption." With large amounts of nectar, the bees can gather lots in a short time. Nectar is their raw material for honey, so lots means cheap. Canola honey causes problems, however. Both the bees and the beekeepers must work around these issues of this genetically modified product.

Canola is a good crop for honey bees, offering both nectar and pollen in early spring. Huge acreages of it are planted in Canada (Alberta, Manitoba, and Saskatchewan) and in North Dakota and Minnesota in the USA. The nectar flows are heavy and yield huge crops of light-colored, mild-flavored honey.

However, rapeseed honey—commonly called canola honey—crystallizes so quickly that it is a problem for beekeepers. It will crystallize in the comb while still in the field! Many beekeepers go through their hives and pull out the combs of canola honey as soon as it is capped. After collecting, it should be extracted within 24 hours and marketed immediately. Extracted canola may last three to four weeks before it crystallizes in the jar. No wonder my bees wouldn't eat this genetically modified stuff. Even though it is cheap, it is of poor quality. It made a mess of my feeders.

You may ask, "What does all this have to do with people exiting the Church?" When people choose to exit Church it is a symptom of something more serious. My bees are naturally attracted to their natural food, but when they don't want to stick around and eat it, something is wrong. A healthy and viable Christian should want to be part of the Christian body. So what may be wrong? Why won't they eat?

As a Christian, what am I feeding on? And as a pastor, what are you feeding? As Christians, we need to take responsibility for our Christian health and get back to the basics of good nutrition. As a beekeeper, I am not off the hook. I have found that it is important to be aware of what I am feeding my bees. Health is a two-way street—feeding and eating. We are in this thing together, so do your part and discern what is going on in the body.

In defense of your pastor: the pastor may only be feeding his "bees" for about 20–30 minutes per week on Sunday morning—even less if you choose to not attend on Sunday morning. Does this mean you are not going to eat for the rest of the week? Even worse, if you don't attend Church at all then are you not eating at all? Try it some time, a great weight loss program. Think about it! How much "pure" scripture do you eat each day or week?

An even bigger mystery: any beekeeper knows that the natural tendency and characteristics of the bees is their drive to be included as a participant of the hive. Thousands of bees all want to be part of their hive. You can't keep them away. Try it sometime. You will get stung. If this is the case, then what excuse does a Christian have for not wanting to be part of a hive of Christians? The only reason: disease is present.

If we are what we eat, then consider the results of this survey; in a survey of 2,900 Christians, when asked how often they personally (not as part of a Church worship service) read the Bible, these were their responses: "Every day" (19 percent) –

"Rarely/Never" (18 percent). A quarter indicated they read the Bible a few times a week. Fourteen percent said they read the Bible "Once a week" and another 22 percent said, "Once a month" or "A few times a month." In a survey of almost 3,000 Evangelical Christians nationwide only 19 percent of them said they feed on God's Word every day. That leaves 81 percent who feed rarely or never. So what are they using for their filter to control what is entering their heart and mind?

We have lots of voices out there sending information into our ears. I was drawn face-to-face with this when I recently upgraded my Bible software. It comes with hundreds of commentaries. A commentary is an interpretation of a scripture as run through another theologian's filter. A host of sermons are available from various teachers, again from a varied series of filters. Many translations of the Bible are available for both Catholics and Protestants. Oh, by the way it also included a copy of the Bible. I use the Bible software often, but the background options are tools, they are not the Word of God.

There are hundreds or perhaps thousands of Christian books on the market telling us what the Bible is really saying. Some are great and some are very destructive to the uninformed. A new Bible translation is now on the market called the Queen James Bible. A book claiming to be the world's first "gay bible" has been published to coincide with the debate on same-sex marriage. Its editors claim that it is a reworking of the King James Bible, translated in a way that "prevents homophobic misinterpretation of God's Word." Form your own opinion on this translation. I am sure it doesn't come with any bias and is totally in line with the original manuscripts—so the scholars like to say. You be the judge.

This is a great solution. Why didn't I think of this? If you have a lifestyle or habit that is in conflict with scripture then just genetically modify the scripture. All is now good. If you are trying to promote a personal agenda then just tip the scales in your favor. Develop a new personal interpretation of scripture. Genetically modify it. Most people won't know. In fact, most people don't read the scripture anyway. All good.

Add to this that on any given day you can listen to hundreds of preachers and evangelists on the radio or the TV. Listen to them for a day and you are sure to be confused. I know I am. A wide range of interpretations of what the Bible is "really" telling us. Is it any wonder that we are seeing a shift in the character and convictions of modern Christians and ultimately the body of believers? Read this clip from an article in USA TODAY, January 10, 2013. This is a mainstream newspaper:

Americans who believe being gay is a sin are now a minority. A November survey from Nashville-based LifeWay Research found 37 percent of Americans polled said "yes." When asked the question, "According to scripture is homosexual behavior a sin?" the article goes on to say that the trend is definitely in the direction of more leniency and the acceptance of this behavior. Of even greater concern is the increase in the number that don't know whether this behavior is sinful or not. A pastor of a large congregation made the comment that being gay is no more sinful than being left-handed.

For sure we are seeing a shift in the convictions of many Christians. Some of this may be healthy but much of it is not. With the fuzzy margins and the lack of understanding of scripture is it any wonder that the consistency of Church attendance is also under attack?

How about the doctrines of hell and Jesus being the only way to salvation? According to a number of articles, most religious believers, including many Christians, say eternal life is not exclusively for those who accept Christ as their Savior. The question must of course be asked: Are some or many of these deceived into thinking that they are Christians? (See Matthew 7:22-23).

Another article quoted the statistic that 52 percent of Christians do not agree with the doctrines many religions teach, particularly conservative denominations. (My comment: Looking from the other end of what this survey is saying, 48 percent of Christians do not believe in hell and think that there is more than one way to heaven than through the cross and Jesus.)

Wow! What are we feeding ourselves? Remember you are what you are eating. If it isn't the scriptures then what is it? So much time is spent on listening to and reading various "Christian" publications that we are quickly drawn along by some of these popular but false teachings. You cannot have a healthy life with Jesus by not reading his Word. Be careful when listening to what all of the others want you to eat/hear.

It is time for Christians, both in the seats and in the pulpit, to take some action. Perhaps it is time to get back to the pure scripture and put aside the particular Church agendas. When the nursery is on fire it isn't a time to sing your baby a lullaby.

Take heed to what Jesus says: *"Then He said to them, 'Take heed what you hear. With the same measure you use, it will be measured to you'"* (Mark 4:24 NKJV). Read scripture to form your own convictions from God's Word and you will get a certain result. Listen to and read other sources of what others want you to know about *religion/so-called Christianity* and you will get their view and follow the view of others. You may *think* you are feeding on the Word of God, but you will be sadly suffering from malnutrition. This is what I have called Genetically Modified Gospel.

Jesus is saying that the size of the measuring cup you use to measure your intake of scripture will determine your spiritual health. Small cup equals anemic Christians. Or worse yet, those who are falsely under the impression that they are Christians from a new and foreign gospel. What will it be? The choice is yours.

Smell the coffee, Church. Wake up Pastors. The Church has a mission field within its own body. Since Church is meant to be a place for believers then we need to get them healthy and get them onto some good honey. In some cases, we need to get those who are under the impression that they are saved to see the fact that they are not. Some have a form of Christianity and not the life-changing experience of Jesus. Our hives have a problem.

Have you ever really considered the weight of the words in this passage? Read the whole passage of Matthew 7 and then consider these words of Jesus.

> 15 *"Beware of false prophets, who come to you in sheep's clothing, but inwardly they are ravenous wolves.* 16 *You will know them by their fruits. Do men gather grapes from thornbushes or figs from thistles?* 17 *Even so, every good tree bears good fruit, but a bad tree bears bad fruit.* 18 *A good tree cannot bear bad fruit, nor can a bad tree bear good fruit.*
> 19 *Every tree that does not bear good fruit is cut down and thrown into the fire.* 20 *Therefore by their fruits you will know them.* 21 *"Not everyone who says to Me, 'Lord, Lord,' shall enter the kingdom of heaven, but he who does the will of My Father in heaven.* 22 *Many will say to Me in that day, 'Lord, Lord, have we not prophesied in Your name, cast out demons in Your name, and done many wonders in Your name?'* 23 *And then I will declare to them, 'I never knew you; depart from Me, you who practice lawlessness!'"* (Matthew 7:15-23 NKJV).

Pastors, consider the fact that your hives are having some issues. As Jesus says in Matthew 7, you may have some who think they are Christians but have been seduced by some foreign doctrine. Don't look for replacement bees. Get the bees you have healthy.

"Not everyone who says to Me, "Lord, Lord,' shall enter the kingdom of heaven, but he who does the will of My Father in heaven." Our mission field can be as close as those who are deceived and are already in our Churches. What do those who *think* they are saved believe? Recent surveys give us our clues.

Be careful about what you teach. It is a huge temptation to filter what you decide to teach based on a bias or some particular pressing need in the current organization. Be honest and think about this for a minute.

The attendance is down so the board instructs you to focus on Church growth. A form of genetically modified teaching is the solution. Sermons are prepared using interpretations with a bias. A subtle slant or an interpretation of scripture should do the job.

I feel I am the wrong guy to be talking about the need for growth. I have been in business all of my working life. Growth is key in any organization. You cannot stand still in this world. I am either moving forward or backwards—and moving backwards eventually will lead to the organization's death. Businesses fail because they fail to keep pace with their market and eventually just fade away. To be successful you find what your market needs and then fill that hole.

Other big forces play a role in most organizations: pride and ego! Who wants to be the captain of a sinking ship? Not me! The natural drive for the leader of an organization is the need for expansion. Expansion is interpreted as success.

What about Church? The same set of dynamics places pressure on the Church leaders and pastors. Talk to a pastor from another Church at any time. Ask the question, "How is your Church doing?" The reply will invariably come back to include a report on the attendance and the programs and the number of services. There must be some scripture that states to pastors what the optimum size of a Church should be. Many pastors feel they have found the answer: Just a little larger. Doesn't matter if the bees can't fly and are sick as long as the size of the hive is increasing.

Perhaps a change of focus would be in order. Try teaching, mentoring, and encouragement on Church health rather than Church growth. Adjust the feed to the real stuff to get the Christians healthy and the growth will follow. Read the upcoming chapter on sheep. Healthy sheep produce lambs. Sick sheep die. Same with bees.

The finances are suffering because the attendance is down. The teaching now shifts to the "Joy of Giving." A form of genetically modified teaching takes place. Heavy-handed offerings are conducted using genetically modified interpretations of scripture. Sermons are prepared using interpretations with a bias to yield a selfish motive promising to increase the honey production of the bees. False hopes lead to the false idea that if the bees will just give more honey in the correct percentage then the bees will magically have financial prosperity. I have seen the fallout of this type of teaching many times.

I am blessed with the opportunity to assist people that are seeking direction while experiencing financial trouble. More than once have I heard this scenario;

Quote: "My wife and I are experiencing financial struggles. We had saved up $2,500 for a large bill coming due that we cannot miss. We are tithing as we have been taught. One Sunday the evangelist was teaching on "sowing into your need to receive a blessing." We gave the $2,500 into the offering. The bill is now due, and we don't have the money. We have been trying to keep up on our tithes but we are running further into debt each month. Can you help us? We know that you offer personal loans. You are our last resort as the banks and credit cards have shut us down." (Another family is heading for the Exit.)

Quote: "My business has failed and I have lost everything. I still have the appearance that all is well, but everything is gone. I have not told anyone about this, so please keep it confidential. I must leave the Church for personal reasons. It is difficult to be around people that will eventually know I have failed. When I told the pastor that I would be going to a different Church he made a comment to not forget about my tithes before leaving. For sure he didn't understand the real reason I am leaving his Church." (Another family is heading for the Exit.)

These all-too-common scenarios are a direct result of genetically modified teaching.

I am not suggesting for a second that the bees do not give of their honey! It is a responsibility for any New Testament Christian to give. Nothing runs for free, your Church included. If you wish to be a part of something then don't be a freeloader. Your pastor has value, and you like to have a place to gather on Sunday. Your kids need to go to Sunday School. You want to be caring for the unfortunate. As Christians, we have a responsibility to support our Church.

Perhaps we should take our sights off the pastor for a second and get the crosshairs on me and you. We don't need another lesson on tithing. Perhaps we just need to focus on our New Testament responsibility for a minute. This does not mean we give nothing because we are *"under grace."* We are in this thing together and this means we all share the load.

> [41] *"Now Jesus sat opposite the treasury and saw how the people put money into the treasury. And many who were rich put in much.* [42] *Then one poor widow came and threw in two mites, which make a quadrans.* [43] *So He called His disciples to Himself and said to them, 'Assuredly, I say to you that this poor widow has put in more than all those who have given*

to the treasury; [44] *for they all put in out of their abundance, but she out of her poverty put in all that she had, her whole livelihood'"* (Mark 12:41-44 NKJV).

(Note to self: Jesus didn't say, "This is the New Testament. Give the widow her money back.")

"For everyone to whom much is given, from him much will be required; and to whom much has been committed, of him they will ask the more" (Luke 12:48 NKJV).

(Note to self: If I am blessed more, then I should give more.)

[1] *"Now concerning the collection for the saints, as I have given orders to the churches of Galatia, so you must do also:* [2] *On the first day of the week let each one of you lay something aside, storing up as he may prosper, that there be no collections when I come.* [3] *And when I come, whomever you approve by your letters I will send to bear your gift to Jerusalem"* (1 Corinthians 16:1-3 NKJV).

(Note to self: Give a little each payday. Paul didn't want to be ragging on me concerning the "Joy of Giving" when he came to preach.)

[26] *"If anyone among you thinks he is religious, and does not bridle his tongue but deceives his own heart, this one's religion is useless.* [27] *Pure and undefiled religion before God and the Father is this: to visit orphans and widows in their trouble, and to keep oneself unspotted from the world"* (James 1:26-27 NKJV).

(Note to self: The widow may need a little cash.)

Just read what the scripture says and do what you think it means. No interpretations or modifications needed. Even I can understand the above scriptures and others like these. Just follow the directions. I am pretty sure they are talking about giving cash. Perhaps a good slogan may be: GOD DOES NOT BLESS FREELOADERS. (*Maybe I shouldn't say that? Whatever.*)

If we value what God has blessed us with, then we should show it. Giving from a cheerful heart and the principle of Christian generosity is a common theme in the New Testament. It is also a known fact that if people's hearts are right then generosity will follow. Amortization may be a key word here. Whether they believe in the principle of tithing or not, few Christians give away that much money. In 2007, research revealed that just five percent of adults tithed. Since you are getting only five percent with the tithing angle why not back off a bit? Encourage everyone to give a little as they are able, and when they are blessed. A little from everyone, in my estimation, will come to a larger cash flow than 10 percent from only five percent.

This is just a little restaurant napkin figuring here—but do you know how many deals I have made on a napkin? More than a few. I tend to frequent restaurants with paper napkins for this reason. Hard to write on the cloth ones! I don't think this is contrary to scripture, especially if you consider the principles that Paul lays out 2 Corinthians 9:6-7 (NKJV): [6] *"But this I say: He who sows sparingly will also reap sparingly, and he who sows bountifully will also reap bountifully.* [7] *So let each one give as he purposes in his heart, not grudgingly or of necessity; for God loves a cheerful giver."*

It may be contrary to some interpretations, however. Encourage the remaining 95 percent to give something and back off on the *"Law of Tithing"* approach. This may be a better approach than teaching tithing as a New Testament law, especially when the organization needs cash. If this isn't teaching from a selfish motive, then it sure does appear to be the case. Very little teaching on tithing is given when the organization is in revival, but lots of teaching every Sunday when the Church is short on cash. Why? Just a thought.

We don't want to offend anyone so the margins become fuzzy. The foundation of the Church becomes unstable and a sort of warm and fuzzy approach is taken. A form of genetically modified teaching takes place. Sermons are prepared using interpretations with a bias to a selfish outcome. Get the unsaved in the door. Don't preach the Spirit-filled life, and the need for repentance from sin. This will sort of happen all by itself by some weird form of osmosis if we keep them in Church long enough. When we are fashioning Church to "Reach the Lost" and not to feed the bees in the hive, a sort of soft-sell approach is taken. And whatever you do, don't scare the people with the notion that there is a hell.

We wonder why our young adults are sort of in constant motion and wandering from Church to Church. What Church are they a part of? That depends on which Sunday you are asking them. Are they part of a body someplace or do we just assume that they are okay? Come to think of it, are they even aware of the importance of being part of a body of believers? They are torn between the club life on Saturday night and too tired on Sunday morning. Not your kids. Ya, right!

> [33] *"Do not be deceived: 'Evil company corrupts good habits.'*
> [34] *Awake to righteousness, and do not sin; for some do not have the knowledge of God. I speak this to your shame"* (1 Corinthians 15:33-34 NKJV).

If our young are not in Church then where do they meet their friends and form their peer group? I heard that young people are interested in dating and looking for a potential mate some day. If they are not part of a Christian body, where do they meet Mr. or Miss Right? The Bar? The Club? It has become more common for Christians to be marrying non-Christians. Even worse, it is becoming more common for the young to just move in together. Yes, even Church youth! Is this any wonder? We assume that they are okay, that they are probably just visiting another Church someplace. Don't just assume this. Is this because we have set up "Fuzzy Margins"?

This type of roaming instinct for the young also has fallout for the parents. Have you ever noticed that once the kids move on, the parents in many cases also vanish? (Another family is heading for the Exit.)

So what is the solution to all of this? To start off, stay true to the gospel message of Jesus. Stay clear of interpretations of scripture that stem from some motive other than the building up of the believers. This applies to both the pastor and the average guy. Just like a family. Build each other up with direction as required.

> [13] *"Now may the God of hope fill you with all joy and peace*
> *in believing, that you may abound in hope by the power of*
> *the Holy Spirit.* [14] *Now I myself am confident concerning you,*
> *my brethren, that you also are full of goodness, filled with all*
> *knowledge, able also to admonish one another.* [15] *Nevertheless,*
> *brethren, I have written more boldly to you on some points,*
> *as reminding you, because of the grace given to me by God,*
> [16] *that I might be a minister of Jesus Christ to the Gentiles,*
> *ministering the gospel of God, that the offering of the Gentiles*
> *might be acceptable, sanctified by the Holy Spirit.* [17] *Therefore*
> *I have reason to glory in Christ Jesus in the things which*
> *pertain to God.* [18] *For I will not dare to speak of any of those*
> *things which Christ has not accomplished through me, in*

word and deed, to make the Gentiles obedient— [19] *in mighty signs and wonders, by the power of the Spirit of God, so that from Jerusalem and round about to Illyricum I have fully preached the gospel of Christ"* (Romans 15:13-19 NKJV).

- ✓ Bless those who are around you.
- ✓ Be full of hope by the power of the Holy Spirit.
- ✓ Be confident that with knowledge of the pure gospel we are able to admonish each other. *Admonish* is a cool word. It doesn't mean criticizing or beating up on each other. Just some strong encouragement.
- ✓ Don't speak about things that we don't know to be true by experience. Stay away from theological theories.
- ✓ Preach the full gospel of Jesus. Leave out the genetically modified stuff.
- ✓ Stick to the pure food of the gospel.

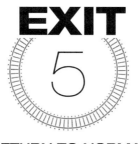

EXIT 5

RETURN TO NORMAL

Why We Lack Understanding:

> *"He commanded them that they should tell no one the things they had seen, till the Son of Man had risen from the dead"* (Mark 9:9 NKJV).

Silence is golden, as the expression goes. All too often we tend to forget this fact. Until we truly understand what Jesus taught we should listen and not speak. We need to exercise caution to not teach until we understand what Christ has taught. Learning the teachings of Jesus—truly learning them with our hearts—takes time. We need to be patient and study his Word to make certain that we are following his instructions to the letter.

Jesus said these words: *"I still have many things to say to you, but you cannot bear them now"* (John 16:12 NKJV).

Jesus is teaching his disciples that learning is a process that involves building upon what we have previously learned. Have you noticed the fact that no matter how many times you read a certain portion of scripture, new truths are still revealed? This is what Jesus is teaching us. His Word is gradually revealed to us. In fact, we were not able to understand them before because we had not yet developed the proper spiritual condition to deal with them. Our foundation was not complete. God doesn't deliberately hide these things from us, but we are not prepared to receive them until we are in the right condition in our spiritual life.

So what is "normal" for a Christian? The Holy Spirit is revealing the meaning of scripture to us. Normal is not reading scripture with an attempt to prove a predetermined agenda for selfish motives. If we have a predetermined agenda then this agenda will, in fact, prevent us from learning what it is that God wants us to learn. Normal is not substituting the reading of scripture with the reading of other writings *about* the Bible. Learn what it is that God has for you. Don't rely on learning what you think God has for you by filtering it through another predigested version.

The following thoughts are from *My Utmost for His Highest: Updated Edition* (Discovery House Publishers, 1992) by Oswald Chambers.

"We must have a oneness with His risen life before we are prepared to hear any particular truth from Him. Do we really know anything about the indwelling of the risen life of Jesus? The evidence that we do is that His Word is becoming understandable to us. God cannot reveal anything to us if we don't have His Spirit. And our own unyielding and headstrong opinions will effectively prevent God from revealing anything to us. But our insensible thinking will end immediately once His resurrection life has its way with us. '…tell no one…' But so many people do tell what they saw on the Mount of Transfiguration—their mountaintop experience. They have seen a vision and they testify to it, but there is no connection between what they say and how they live."

Now read 2 Corinthians 3:1-18.

- ✓ Clearly you are an epistle (a letter) of Christ written not with ink but by the Spirit of the living God, not on tablets of stone but on tablets of flesh, that is, of the heart.

- ✓ Our sufficiency is from God.
- ✓ After Moses' meeting with God on the mountain the children of Israel could not look steadily at his face because of the glory of his countenance, which glory was passing away. So Moses put a veil over his face because the children of Israel could not look at him otherwise. (Note: This was a process of change and eventually passing away.)
- ✓ Nevertheless when one turns to the Lord, the veil is taken away. (It takes the presence of Jesus to help us see past the veil.)
- ✓ Now the Lord is the Spirit; and where the Spirit of the Lord is, there is liberty.
- ✓ Beholding as in a mirror the glory of the Lord, we are being transformed into the same image. (We are to look forward to being a reflection of the image of Jesus.)

For any change to take place it must start with individuals—you and me. The change that I really want and need is to see the reflection of Jesus looking back at me when I gaze into a mirror. Unfortunately, or fortunately, this state of change is not a static process. This is very well illustrated in the passages of 2 Corinthians chapter 3. Moses went up the mountain to have a face-to-face meeting with God. Can you imagine being a fly on the wall at that meeting? To say the least, Moses was transformed by this meeting, and even his appearance was altered by the presence of God. It was manifested on his face. The brightness of God was so intense that they had to put a cloth over his face because their eyesight would have been damaged if they merely looked at the reflection of God on his face.

If this condition had lasted forever, it would have become normal. We are told, however, that this condition was already changing shortly after his return to the flatlands below. For a brief time the glory of the Lord was shining on his face, but as we know, eventually they could take the cloth from his face and they could once again look at him.

Moses had a life-changing spiritual experience and it became the strength that he needed to continue to lead the Church to places that God wanted them to travel to. This experience was the catalyst to get things moving in the right direction, but Moses could not spend the rest of his life with his head in a sack. The modern Church is no different. We need a jumpstart from Jesus to get back to normal.

Now fast-forward to the present age and the modern local Church. Are you, as a member of "the Church," exempt from the above passages? Are the current Church leaders exempt? Even our pastors need this mountaintop experience to determine what the eventual "normal" will be for them. Until our pastors also experience this mountaintop transformation then not much will change.

Now back to our question at hand: The man whom I was standing beside leaned over and asked me, "Is it always like this?" I thought that he was impressed by the activities and enthusiasm over what was taking place. I decided to ask him to explain his question.

This question is subject to a particular reference in time and spiritual condition.

1. This would be a positive question if the Spirit of Lord is present and this is the current normal we are witnessing. (A good normal)
2. This is a negative question if the Spirit of the Lord is not present and the empty activities have become our normal so that we can get our attendance card checked as "present at Church" for another week. (A bad normal - not very healthy)

According to a 2007 Gallup survey, "In Canada, Australia, and countries in Europe, such as the UK, less than 20% of the population may attend religious services every week." I heard another comment that the average attendance for evangelical Church members is about nine times per year or about once every five weeks.

Now let me ask you what *your* normal is, and ask you if you are you willing to change. The opening of this chapter may appear to give the impression that I am placing the full responsibility on pastors. Not so. If change is to take place and the Church is to get back to normal, then it may mean that even I may need to change. You as well. Change starts with the guy looking back at us from the mirror. Our reflection must begin to resemble Christ. Our spirit is to be in sync with the spirit of the risen Jesus. Normal is not a time or place, but our relationship with Jesus.

I am going to work on what my view of normal is. Bear in mind that "normal" is not a static condition. Just as with Moses it is not a lasting "mountaintop" experience with my head in a sack. My analogy to emphasize this point will involve two men. Our two identical men are both 40 years old, both professional men in their area, but in different parts of the world.

Man number one is a lawyer complete with a suit and tie in downtown Vancouver, Canada. He lives in an upscale neighborhood and usually eats his lunch at one of the finer restaurants in downtown Vancouver. Come to think of it, this guy is most likely overweight from constantly eating restaurant food.

Man number two lives in the jungles of Borneo, complete with a loin cloth. His work does not have a jacket and tie policy. He eats on the job, looking for bugs and roots to feed his family. He has bugs and roots for lunch. Come to think of it, he is not overweight. Bugs aren't fattening.

Both men are living their *normal* life style. But what happens if you buy them each a plane ticket and have them transported to the other's home? Sort of an exchange student program. Each man's normal suddenly becomes *not* normal for the other guy. Get my point?

My point is: I have to be conscious of the fact that normal for someone else may not be normal for me. I have to seek God to find what God's normal is for my life, and then seek God to start the transition from my unhealthy and unspiritual normal. My new normal may commence with a mountaintop experience, but eventually I will need to remove the sack from my head and come back down to earth to be effective. A normal that is not according to God's plan soon becomes aimless apathy. Are we there yet?

Have you ever met one of those people that try to maintain a "super spiritual mode"? I think we need to give a caution about this as well. Be real but not phony. This is sometimes one of the hazards when a person is attempting to change to the spiritual mode, but is trying to do it under their own steam. They appear spiritual but drive everyone nuts! In reality, the transition will be a process but should be sustainable—and shouldn't bug others.

Epilogue: The man from Borneo stepped off the airplane at Vancouver International Airport and got smoked by a bus. The lawyer was eaten by some exotic animal from the jungle. A native in Borneo was later found wearing a red tie as a loin cloth.

I need to change my understanding of normal. What is my definition of normal? Is it some experience in the past, which is limited depending on my past experiences? Or is it a condition that God intended for me to move forward to? As I understand it, normal is a heart condition and not a geographic position.

Cherril and I recently took a flight for a vacation to Hawaii. We are traveling at 36,000 feet and an air speed of 465 knots. We like to have the assurance that everything is normal when the pilot comes on the intercom with his welcoming remarks and the weather report for our destination. What does normal mean?

Now go back in time to December of 1903. The Wright brothers were still trying to get off the ground and they succeeded. What was normal in 1903?

On December 17, 1903, Orville Wright piloted the first powered airplane 20 feet above a wind-swept beach in North Carolina. The flight lasted 12 seconds and covered 120 feet. Three more flights were made that day with Orville's brother Wilbur piloting the record flight lasting 59 seconds over a distance of 852 feet. [www.eyewitnesstohistory.com]

If we go back to 1903 then what our modern-day pilot is telling us is taking place is downright frightening, even to the Wright brothers. Their reference point was not being able to fly at all the day before.

Now go back to 1917 and fly in a high tech aircraft for that day, a high-powered and high-performance double-wing aircraft. I would like to say a Sopwith Camel (top speed 103 knots, its maximum range 300 miles) but I can't because that plane could only transport one person, the pilot.

You climb in the back seat—they didn't have back seats back then, but just pretend. Did they have seat belts then? You place the leather aviator's helmet on, adjust your goggles and scarf. You take off and your scarf is now flying in the wind. You are in the rear seat and the pilot comes on the intercom…Oops! Intercoms were not normal for that time period. He turns around and yells at you with this report:

- ✓ We will be climbing to 36,000 feet for our cruising altitude. (You know, however, that there is barely any oxygen up there! Even the pilot will lose consciousness in about five minutes at about 22,000 feet.) Not to worry, however: our pilot has big lungs.

- ✓ We will be increasing our speed to 465 knots. (You know the wings will blow off this old bird at about 150 knots, and you can only reach this air speed in a full dive.)
- ✓ Our estimated flight time to Hawaii will be about 27 hours. (You know that this old bird can only hold enough gas to stay in the air for about three hours!) Not a problem, however; our plan is that the pilot has scheduled nine fuel stops as we cross the Pacific. "Where!!??" you ask!!!!!
- ✓ You YELL (actually, *SCREAM* in terror) back at the pilot that you are going into full heart failure!
- ✓ The pilot yells back to not be concerned, assuring you that "Everything is normal" in his calm baritone airline pilot voice.

Does your heart rate then return back to normal? Actually, on this thought, what *is* your normal heart rate, and what emotions do you feel if you go to the doctor and he says your heart is not functioning normally. I wonder why?

Sometimes I lose my way when I am trying to determine what it is that God wants me to be for today. I like to go back in my mind to those good old days at camp, when the Spirit of the Lord was so powerful. That was a good normal for then but even as a kid, it wasn't sustainable. I couldn't stay at camp.

Don't forget that normal is not static. Normal is fluid depending on the time and circumstances and your view point. All we need to do is look around and we will see that this statement is true. Very little in this world remains constant. Just look at your own body in the mirror. This is normal for *today*.

Now (depending on your age) look at a picture of yourself 20 years ago. That was normal for you then. Has very much changed? If you are a man reading this, you could see your feet and you had hair back then. (Scary how much "normal" can change in a short time.) As for ladies…no, I believe I will stay clear of what is your body's "normal."

In many of life's experiences we see that normal, in fact, may be a deteriorating condition. In our walk with Jesus, however, we want this to be a growing experience. Each day's normal should be better than the previous day. Is that what you are experiencing? Why or why not?

What I need to do is establish a new constant for my new and personal spiritual "normal." My new normal needs to reflect this truth: *"The Lord is the Spirit; and where the Spirit of the Lord is, there is liberty…beholding as in a mirror the glory of the Lord, [we] are being transformed into the same image"* (2 Corinthians 3:17-18 NKJV). If this is not the case then I have a problem and need to start seeking God to start his change in me to get me fast-forwarded back to normal. Do you notice that it is fast-*forward* to normal, because we cannot go backwards? We need to move forward to where Jesus is standing and stop looking backwards.

Many times we have heard the expression if we could just get back to the apostolic age, then all would be good. Many books have suggested that this is the place that the Church should try to get back to. The first century Church. Wrong! We would still be in the same rut with the same old heart condition.

How do I know what Church should be like, if I don't first understand what Church is meant to be? What is Church? Think about this for a moment, and see if you can write down an answer to this question. Not much point in trying to come *back* to something, or move *forward* to it, if I don't know what I am trying to move towards.

What if God came to you this morning, and spoke face to face and audibly to you? He says to you, "I have chosen to grant you one wish. Think on this carefully. I will move you and the Church to any point in time that you request. Both you and the "normal"

Church will be restored to the "normal" spiritual condition that my people are enjoying at that time."

You know that this is a once-in-a-lifetime chance, and your decision is a pivotal decision that will affect your future spiritual condition and the future of the Church for eternity. What will your request be and what time period would this be? Wow! No pressure here! Remember, you are speaking to God, and he for sure has the power to grant your request!

Keep thinking on this question; we'll come back to the answer a bit later. (I need some time to come up with the correct answer for this! I'm going to drive my wife nuts with this one, for sure.)

We have a huge problem in finding the answer to this question, and I think the problem is increasing rather than coming closer to a solution. That's because our perspective of normal is not God's normal. The lens we are looking through is not set to the same resolution as God's lens. In actual fact, the resolution of our lens becomes poorer in quality each day and it is not just due to eyesight. As the older people die off, and the younger people move into the places of Church leadership, the Church normal (based on past experiences) will shift.

The old guys love to look back to the good old days. But even the oldest of the old guys cannot go back more than 100 years. Has anyone reading this had a flight in a Sopwith Camel? What did we have 100 years ago, when we are looking for firsthand experience as a point to return to? Anything past even 75 years is a stretch, subject to memory loss of the old guys…and on *this* data we are asked to make a decision that will change the history of the Church? Now contemplate further your answer to God's offer. This is the best case scenario that you can personally relate to—a 100-year window at best!

Okay, young guys. Hold your horses for a minute. Here comes the part where the old guys bash the young guys. (Settle down for a minute. This won't hurt a bit.) Consider that the ages of our current potential Church leaders are more in the 30–40 age range. What definition does their lens provide? What is their normal? For the Church to return to normal, we need to define what that is. What are the old guys giving the young guys to increase their perspective?

What about it, old guys? What are you doing to stay engaged with the young guys? Are you looking at life through their lenses or are you just beating on them because their normal may not be exactly what your normal is?

The old guys sometimes look with disdain at the young guys that are moving into Church leadership. Suck it up, old guys! This is the real world. Don't forget *your* age when you became active in Church leadership. My first term as a Church deacon was when I was around 35 years old. My pastor at that time was about 40. Those were the good old days. The camp speakers of the day were about 30–45 max.

My son-in-law, Tim, is a paramedic for the B.C. Ambulance Service—a great guy, and a hard worker, and someone who knows his stuff. He is currently studying to know even more. He just had his twenty-eighth birthday. Young guy, you say? Nice kid. You will sure be glad to have him show up if that OLD ticker knocks you to the deck some day. Don't discredit youth. Age doesn't have anything to do with normal, but a good "benchmark" does, young guys and old guys included.

Martin Luther was only 34 years old when he posted his *Ninety-Five Theses* on October 31, 1517. This is not a typo. Almost 500 years ago. I don't think most Christians even know what the Ninety-Five Theses were all about…or for that fact, who is Martin Luther? If you are not a Catholic, then arguably one of the key players in your Church history as a Protestant is Martin Luther. If you are Catholic, then arguably Martin Luther is one of the key players that helped bring reformation to the Catholic Church. This guy caused a real dust-up in the Church world. In 1517 the normal Church was pretty sick for any believer. For sure we would not want to return to the year 1500 to find normal.

When you mention Martin Luther it is very common for him to be confused with Martin Luther King. "Who is *he*?" you may ask. Wow! As the lawyers say in court, "I rest my case." Look up "Martin Luther Ninety-Five Theses on 31 October 1517." This was a very key document to move the Church forward and closer to normal.

We need to have a benchmark to measure from. Did you know that even the term "benchmark" is a precise term in engineering and construction? In navigation, the term "datum" applies to the same principle but is more precise and even further outside of the box.

Many new cars have a GPS system installed. Did you know that your car's GPS system will not even work without the benchmark or datum that is precisely entered for you when you start your car? I think this term deserves a definition seeing as how we sort of stumbled on it. In actual fact, our pilot in the example above will be relying heavily on the datum in order to not get lost. If our pilot knows where he is, this is a good thing when you're halfway across the Pacific! A pretty important term!

What is a "***benchmark***"?

The term bench mark originates from the chiseled horizontal marks that surveyors made in stone structures, into which an angle-iron could be placed to form a "bench" for a leveling rod, thus ensuring that a leveling rod could be accurately repositioned in the same place in the future. The term is generally applied to any item used to mark a point as an elevation reference. Frequently, bronze or aluminum disks are set in stone or concrete, or on rods driven deeply into the earth to provide a stable elevation point. [From the Wikipedia article, "benchmark," accessed July 3, 2013]

Now, try to agree on one answer for that perfect particular point in time that you would like to move to. You all need to have 100 percent agreement on this point in time to have your request to God be granted and achieve the perfect Church.

But remember, people have very different ideas of what "the perfect Church" is. How about the person who just became a Christian in the last week? How about the friend who comes from a different geographic area? How about the friend who has a background from a different denomination than yours? You get the picture. You all are looking through different lenses but you must have full 100 percent agreement. Sounds simple enough. Why not email this question to a few friends and see what happens?

To further define a "benchmark" and assist us in returning to the "normal Church" I mentioned that a benchmark is a point of reference to work to or from. In some cases we need a more accurate reference point than in other cases. The Church may be one of these examples. We must have a point of reference that is outside of ourselves, and his name is Jesus.

In construction, you sometimes are given the benchmark for the required level of the main floor above the center line of the front street. This is easy: you take the measurement of the height of the street, and you set your foundation level at the required height, to make sure that your main floor will not be any lower than the street elevation.

Many times when Christians are trying to seek an elevation for their Church they set a benchmark that is the same as their Church was back in 1964 at a particular address. Or if we are looking for a more current model, we send out spies and then say that if we are like this current Church "someplace" then we will see Church growth. If we change our music and technology to be like this Church then we will be on the road to success. What is success, by the way?

On a recent trip to the Hawaiian island of Kauai, I got talking to someone in construction and heard of an interesting benchmark requirement. In one particular area, a building could not be constructed any higher than the "highest palm tree in the neighborhood." It's an interesting concept, but difficult to apply when building in Langley, B.C. in the winter with a foot of snow. Hard to locate the highest palm tree in Langley.

Many times we need something a little more accurate than palm trees and road elevations. Take our pilot example. The passengers may get a bit anxious if his trip across the Pacific was only required to maintain an altitude higher than the palm trees in the area. Great views for the passengers, but not all that practical. A more precise calculation would be based on maintaining an elevation relative to sea level. This is a known level, but even that can fluctuate according to tides, as we have previously learned. You get the point.

What about my Christian life, and—more to the theme of this book—what am I using as our benchmark for my walk with the Lord? What is the benchmark for establishing the purpose and mission of our Church, or what is our Church hoping to achieve as its mission statement? We need something far more definitive than just looking back to the Church of Acts, or the apostolic age. Sounds great, sells books, but that is about it. Our benchmark must be the right position of my heart in relation to Jesus. After all, the Church is his body and not the first Church of Acts.

Is the benchmark for our "perfect Church" another Church that we are aware of? Sort of the palm tree concept. Is the "perfect Church" one that we can recall in the backroom of our mind from some previous day—sort of the sea level concept or the center of the road idea? Not the most reliable benchmarks for something so important. At the very least, this limits how much God is allowed to move in our lives.

Perhaps we as Christians need to look outside of the box—perhaps our pastors and Church leaders also need to look outside of the box—a bit higher than the palm trees when we make our request or wish known to God.

What is your benchmark now for returning to normal? Time for a bonus round. Let's reinforce this concept of establishing a benchmark. Come back to our fictitious offer from God for a minute.

What if God came to you this morning, and spoke face to face and audibly to you. He says to you, "I have chosen to grant you one wish. Think on this carefully. I will move you and the Church to any point in time that you request. Both you and the 'normal' Church will be restored to the 'normal' spiritual condition that my people are enjoying at that time."

Now let's make this decision a little more difficult. (I intend to try this myself with a group of friends.) Gather together about a dozen people that you know well, but come from different backgrounds and have different life experiences. Also, vary the ages from young to old.

EXIT 6

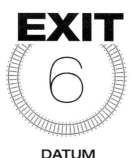

DATUM

Have you ever been lost? I don't mean momentarily losing your car at the mall or being unable to find the Food Court. I mean really seriously lost! Those unfortunate people that spend their recreation time in the city really miss out. Lots of great experiences come from camping, boating, hunting, and fishing. I have had my fair share.

This morning I asked my wife if she remembers the time we were on the boat and we got lost in the fog. Welcome to a day in the life of Cherril when her reply was, "Which time are you talking about?" She is adjusting well to these adventures. As it turns out she missed this particular experience I am going to use for this illustration. However, she has been with me on some other learning experiences. This should give some clarity to the term, "datum." I wasn't really lost. I just didn't know where I was, other than on the boat.

A definition to get us started. These are all good things to know when you are lost.

A geodetic datum is a reference point from which measurements are made. In surveying and navigation, a datum is a set of reference points against which position measurements are made. Horizontal datums are used for describing a point on the Earth's surface, in latitude and longitude. Vertical datums measure elevations or depths. [From the Wikipedia article, "datum," accessed July 3, 2013.]

Short Form: Datum is a precise point outside of your box to use as your reference. When lost, you don't need to travel to the datum; you just need to know where it is. Any thoughts as to what this could be for a Christian?

A friend of mine is a surveyor, and he received a contract a number of years ago to establish a datum in Langley, B.C. as part of the National Geodetic Survey being conducted at that time. This is big stuff, and really working outside of the box. In order to have accurate survey data and navigational data, including data for maps, you need to have a precise and known reference. This takes "precise" to a whole new level and well beyond your local house address or the mall parking lot. In order to know where you are, or where you are going, you need a reference that is in relation to something that is not variable—a landmark, so to speak, or perhaps something a bit higher than a landmark.

My friend the surveyor set up camp at the chosen location in Langley and established a "mark" at the desired location. Doesn't sound that complicated: he pounded a stick in the ground. He then needed to establish the precise location of the mark. A stake in the middle of a field on 196th Street wasn't close enough. You may locate it with that description if you are familiar with the field, but you couldn't navigate around the world or draw maps or surveys in Calgary using that definition as a location.

It took my friend about two weeks camping in this field to identify the exact location and elevation of the stake in the ground. He needed to have some point of reference that was greater than a point on the Earth. His task was to pinpoint this stake in relation to the North Star and other celestial bodies. If the night was cloudy and he couldn't see the stars then work was suspended.

Ancient explorers knew the necessity of working from a datum that was outside of themselves. They set off to find new lands. Finding new lands was great, but it was also a bonus if they could find their way back home to tell the king. Have you ever wondered how they found their way back home? Remember they had no maps because nobody had ever been there before! They had some very basic instruments, but these instruments are still in use today and very accurate by the way—such as a compass that uses the north magnetic pole of the Earth as an earthly datum (But even this moves from year to year. Bet you didn't know that.) A datum outside of our Earth is measured by a sextant that tells the location of the North Star and other stars, the moon and the sun, in relation to a point on the Earth. These appear to be fixed in space in a position relative to the Earth. Pretty cool. Some appear to move in perfect time for a reason, and some appear to be stationery in the skies also for a specific reason.

When you turn on your car's direction system (Global Positioning System), which you can buy at Costco for about $150 bucks, do you have any idea how the technology in that little box works? It first needs to locate its datum, the reference satellite about 37,000 nautical miles above the Earth. After some technological magic, it tells you that you are at the mall and how to get home. My daughter has a directional handicap and she uses this magic frequently.

How does the satellite datum know its location? You guessed it: it is in relation to the heavens and the stars which are measured as light years above the Earth. For hundreds of years, smart people knew that God hung the objects of space in precise locations. This fact now enables a GPS system to be precise within millimeters for any point on Earth. It also works for any aircraft in the sky or any rocket in space.

Now if *that* doesn't start to get our thinking outside of the box, read this. It is amazing that the old explorers on a sailing ship knew this, navigators and surveyors know this, but many Christians don't know that we need a datum that is outside of their personal environment, region, and time. Small wonder that they are influenced in countless different directions by shifting worldly trends around them.

> [1] *"The heavens declare the glory of God; and the firmament shows His handiwork.* [2] *Day unto day utters speech, and night unto night reveals knowledge.* [3] *There is no speech nor language where their voice is not heard.* [4] *Their line has gone out through all the earth, and their words to the end of the world. In them He has set a tabernacle for the sun,* [5] *which is like a bridegroom coming out of his chamber, and rejoices like a strong man to run its race.* [6] *Its rising is from one end of heaven, and its circuit to the other end; and there is nothing hidden from its heat.* [7] *The law of the Lord is perfect, converting the soul; the testimony of the Lord is sure, making wise the simple;* [8] *the statutes of the Lord are right, rejoicing the heart; the commandment of the Lord is pure, enlightening the eyes;* [9] *the fear of the Lord is clean, enduring forever; The judgments of the Lord are true and righteous altogether"* (Psalms 19:1-9 NKJV).

According to the title, David is the author of Psalm 19. It appears that even David, way back in 1000 BC, understood the heavens and the stars and planets.

How does all this relate to the question we are trying to answer about Exits? Why are people exiting the Church? Perhaps part of the challenge is that many of us that make up the Church, starting with the pastor and working down the attendance list, have lost our datum. In the previous chapter we learned about a "benchmark" which is established in relation to datum. Perhaps these missing-in-action believers have even lost their benchmark—which is even less precise.

If we don't recognize the fact that people are exiting then we are blind. It is not just the average Church attendee either. I can understand a pastor deciding to leave working within the Church structure to retire or to enter some other form of work. I appreciate pastors. They have a difficult job, in my opinion. Try working for an organization that is made up of a group of people that have different ideas about what the "perfect Church" looks like, and who all feel that they are your employer. This could be why some pastors are choosing to change their vocation. This doesn't explain, however, why some pastors choose to not attend *any* Church, but leave the Church altogether. They are still Christians, but not connected with a local Church. This is not that uncommon. Do you know anyone that has gone "missing in action" from the Church, even a former pastor? I do.

Some leaving the Church are not actually leaving suddenly, but are in a state of drift until they become missing from the Church. I think a good term for this would be "Spiritual Drift." They do not make a conscious decision to grow cold towards the Lord. I think in most cases this is a gradual process, or drifting to a colder place. This is much like letting the mooring lines loose from a boat tied at the dock during mild weather. The boat moves ever so slowly but over the course of the day the boat can be a long way from the safety of the dock. This same effect is even the case with huge ocean-going vessels. Spiritual Drifting is very similar.

Another challenge is the fact in many Churches, the act of drifting may not even be apparent. We have become so accustomed to not seeing people on a regular basis that, when they finally stop attending altogether, we don't even know they are missing. As previously noted, according to a 2007 Gallup survey, in Canada, less than 20 percent of the population may attend religious services every week and the average member of a Church may attend once every five weeks.

This would make an interesting computer model. Take 250 people and place them in a computer model that cycles every member once every five weeks. How often would these people actually bump into each other? Add to this the growing trend of two services on Sunday. The Church is not full, and seating is for sure not an issue, but the current model for many Churches is for two services. This would be like having the average family of four attending meals at various sittings, the 4:00 p.m. meal or the 6:00 p.m. meal, or just drop in for a snack. Get my point? Many people who are part of the "body of believers" hardly see each other. This not bumping into each other is similar to a dysfunctional family. Certain characteristics seem to be common in dysfunctional families—the first being that they rarely have meals together. The fridge is sort of like a locker in the middle of the kitchen that serves as a feeding station. They experience very little down time together, rarely have communication with each other, and sort of eat on the run.

Once a Christian or a Church loses its datum then drifting commences. Without a point of reference you do not even know you are drifting. It just sort of happens gradually.

I think this is a good point to insert my "Lost in the Fog" story. The time frame is prior to all this fancy technology that you can now buy for about $150. We spent the summer up north and it was time to move our boat home to its home port near Vancouver. For some reason, my wife was not onboard so I was making the last leg of the trip of about 125 miles solo. Sounds like the opening of Gilligan's Island "for a three-hour cruise." (Do you young guys even know who Gilligan is?) The anticipated trip would have taken about eight hours if all had gone well.

Just over halfway to my destination I encountered fog. I radioed the coast guard, and listened to the updated weather report: "Patchy fog, average visibility two miles, moderate sea conditions." No big deal. Patchy is nothing. This means fog for a short while and then clear patches for a while. Done this hundreds of times. Check the charts; plot my position and intended course for the last 50 miles. Set my speed for fog at 10 knots so I can keep track of my progress as one mile every six minutes and then update my positions on the chart. In the old days they called this "dead reckoning." I still am not all the comfortable with combining the word "dead" with boating or flying. Nevertheless, I still know how to do this.

The term "patchy" turned out to be subjective. After about an hour the clear part never happened, but the visibility part reduced to about ZERO. I had no reference to gauge the distance. I couldn't see a thing. The bow of the boat was barely visible. No big deal. My boat's compass was working well so all was well. Not a problem. I should be in clear skies any moment… Not true. Visibility remained at zero. I maintained my intended course and speed and updated my position on my chart every eighteen minutes as three miles. I had a pretty good idea where I was. Dead reckoning again. Great nautical term.

I wasn't really lost. I just didn't know exactly where I was. By the time I knew I was approximately 30 miles from my destination but without any external reference or land marks, I was literally traveling blind. I relied on my experience and what I knew but I needed to locate some point of reference to re-establish my known position on the chart. Once I got close to land, it would be a good idea to know when I would hit the beach. A good thing to know! Boats don't float on rocks.

Now for the awesome part, and to establish my known position and a safe course to home. This is how important a known DATUM is and how to locate it when lost. Compared to my previous chapter on benchmarks, I was way past the point of looking for the "highest palm tree" on the beach.

The work that my buddy did when he did the survey in Langley years ago, paid off. He most likely never knew that someday I would need it.

I radioed Vancouver Marine Traffic and told them my situation and approximate location, direction, and water speed. I knew this because of "dead reckoning." Their instructions were to hold my radio mike open and count up to 10 and backwards to zero. They were able to locate the source of my radio signal and establish my position according to a known datum. Once this was done, they were able to locate me on radar and distinguish me as a target from other boats in the area...and palm trees. They now identified me as a known target on radar and could follow my progress.

They gave me my exact position and I was able to exactly plot this on my chart. I now knew exactly where I was. Further to this, their instructions were to report in every 30 minutes and they would reconfirm my exact location. With an extra set of eyes, I could now see in the fog. Also other vessels in the area were aware of my location and could avoid bumping into me. This is also good when you can't see.

Remember my term, "DRIFT." On the water is much different than on land. You are traveling in a fluid environment. Not that different than life, really. You can travel in a steady direction (my course) but you may not be going where you think you are going. If you have visibility you can make adjustments for this. The effects of wind and current cause you to drift. Again, not that much different than life. I had drifted about a half mile off course to the north as the current from the tide was pushing me north and the wind was also from the south. Not good when the destination harbor entrance was only about 200 yards wide and about twenty miles ahead.

I could draw this story out a bit longer, but unless you are a boater you may lose interest. If you aren't a boater or outdoor type, hopefully you get the drift. The outcome of the story is that all went well, and this is the kind of experience that keeps outdoor experiences exciting and creates good times and builds experience. I enjoy these types of experiences and Cherril is adjusting well.

Am I drifting or are you drifting? Do you care? Does your Church even know? Just drifting is usually a dangerous condition. It is not any less dangerous when a Christian is drifting and loses their datum. Now that they have lost their datum it is even more of a risk if they are not part of the support of their Church family. Once drifting remains unchecked in a believer's life they don't even realize they are on a course to trouble—especially if a period of prolonged fog settles in. No alarm bells are going off but they just sort of drift over the horizon and disappear. This is not a winning combination for either the drifter or for their Church family.

When you feel yourself starting to drift, take action quickly. You will not have so far to come back from. I don't need to prepare a long list; you will know the symptoms of drifting: the loss of the desire to read your Bible; the loss of the desire to spend time in prayer; the loss of the desire to associate with your Church family. Sound familiar?

EXIT 7

TERRIBLE TWOS!

Now that I have had some fun and driven my friends and family nuts with my question, I should come to some conclusion.

The question was: "What if God came to you this morning, and spoke face to face and audibly to you. He says to you, 'I have chosen to grant you one wish. Think on this carefully. I will move you and the Church to any point in time that you request. Both you and the "normal" Church will be restored to the "normal" spiritual condition that my people are enjoying at that time.'"

To leave a question open and not come to a conclusion is counterproductive to the point of this book. The process, however, has taken me personally in a direction that I did not anticipate when I asked it. Before we go into some of the responses for the perfect Church let's look at a couple of true-life examples in the Bible that may define the perfect Church. Good place to start.

We have all heard of the terrible twos. If you have kids you are well aware of this phenomenon. As freedom comes with being able to walk and communicate, the strong desire to exercise this new freedom emerges in our infant. It can be a trying time to say the least. Unfortunately, this desire to become a free spirit can hit at any age and not just the two-year-olds. Some may hit this wall in their teens and even much later. How often do we hear a senior walking by singing, "Don't Fence Me In"? Some refer to this as Freedom 55 and grandma and grandpa go nuts. They leave town in their RV for months on end. To use the famous words of Martin Luther King Jr.: "Free at last! Free at last! Thank God Almighty, we are free at last."

At any age we hear the excuses such as, "I am just all churched-out. I just want to be free of all of the Church politics." Interesting concept and sounds very spiritual. Sounds like a good reason to be removed from Church.

In Exodus we find a Church of just over 1,200,000 people that is stuck in Egypt in slavery. They have been slaves for over 400 years, and had no leader and no direction. Just stuck making bricks for Pharaoh. It doesn't look like much hope, just bondage. God raises up a leader by the name of Moses, a stirring in the camp is felt, and the First Assembly of Egypt will soon be moving forward to freedom. Most of us know the story found in Exodus. Starting in Exodus 14 we see one instance of the character of a normal Church. They have just been miraculously freed from 400 years of backbreaking labor as slaves. Now they think that God has abandoned them and they are trapped at the Red Sea with Pharaoh's armies bearing down on them.

One of the first things that we see in many Churches is fear of the unknown and complaining. Many ordinary folk are uneasy when they experience the unknown and are asked to move forward to something that is greater. Our sample Church in Exodus, without the strong leadership of Moses, would have headed back to Egypt and gone back to brick-making. It was easier for them in their fearful hearts to go with what they knew—slavery.

The complaining starts in Exodus 14:12 (NKJV): *"For it would have been better for us to serve the Egyptians than that we should die in the wilderness."* How soon we forget! Only a few weeks out of slavery and they have already forgotten how hard life was as slaves to the Egyptian.

Moses gets them over this hurdle and they are amazed that God has a plan and wants to move them forward to something much better than slavery. Just when things looked impossible the second time, God performs another miracle: *"Then Moses stretched out his hand over the sea; and the Lord caused the sea to go back by a strong east wind all that night, and made the sea into dry land, and the waters were divided"* (Exodus 14:21 NKJV). Wow! The sea just dried up and Israel crossed over on dry land.

A dry sea bed is great as long as your enemy is also not chasing after you on the same sea bed. But they were, so once again, God intervenes on Israel's behalf. Time to slow their enemy down for a spell (verse 25). God took over and protected Israel and destroyed their enemy of self-doubt and complaining. I get a chuckle over the way some things are described in scripture. Talk about making it rough on the Egyptians: the wheels even fell off their chariots. Ever try driving with no wheels? Not that good! This slowed the Egyptians down long enough for Israel to get clear of the sea bottom. Once they were all clear, the sea closed in and drowned the Egyptians. God always has a good plan and just in time. If Israel would only settle down and realize this. How about us?

Now our sample Church gets across the Red Sea and is only three months into freedom when they come to Mount Sinai (Exodus 19). Now get this: only three months into freedom and they establish the First Assembly of Sinai, membership 1,200,000. Wow! That is quite a Church plant.

God comes and speaks to the people. God sets the mountaintop on fire. Wow! Lots of smoke and fire. He then tells Moses to head up the mountain into the fire and smoke and have a visit with God. Yeah, right! Lots of trumpet sounds, thunder, and lightning. I don't ever recall any Church dedication this impressive. Even with all of this going on the people still complained and talked about the good old days. Now comes the Terrible Twos with the two-year-olds joining forces with the seniors yelling , "Free at last! Free at last! Thank God Almighty, we are free at last!" Quite a chorus! Their song of praise is right but their actions are wrong. It is almost impossible to imagine that complaining could take place with such an impressive display of God's caring power.

Short attention span this bunch. A major case of A.D.D. While Moses is away the people decide to throw a party and bring in some of their own ideas. Test their newfound freedom. Good grief! How long was Moses away? Not that long. Leave the kids alone for a minute and they will come up with some great plan to improve on what God has in store for them. While God is speaking to Moses, the mountain is on fire with thunder and lightning, and the kids hatch a plan and say, "God has left us. What are we missing here? Let's go back to what we know and not wait for what God has for us." God had a plan for his Church at Sinai but the people had a better plan. Do you think that this is still the case even in our current day Churches?

> [19] *"So it was, as soon as he came near the camp, that he saw the calf and the dancing. So Moses' anger became hot, and he cast the tablets out of his hands and broke them at the foot of the mountain.* [20] *Then he took the calf which they had made, burned it in the fire, and ground it to powder; and he scattered it on the water and made the children of Israel drink it.* [21] *And Moses said to Aaron, 'What did this people do to you that you have brought so great a sin upon them?'"* (Exodus 32:19-21 NKJV).

Moses is ticked off! He gets frustrated and angry with this whole big show. The stupidity and sin of his Church that has become stuck with the past gets the better of Moses. Can I see any similarities to this in my own attitudes and ideas? I want to stick with what I know, go back to what I know rather than change to the exciting plan God has for his Church today and for the future. It comes from thinking that the past was better, but God tells us, *"Do not say, 'Why were the former days better than these?' For you do not inquire wisely concerning this"* (Ecclesiastes 7:10 NKJV). No wonder Moses lost his cool and had a temper tantrum and broke the tablets, the very Word of God for that time. Wow! Sobering thought. Moses was some upset guy, to say the least!

Am I ever thankful that God is patient with us. If I was God, I would have thought that these kids are hopeless. Send them back to Egypt to make bricks. God is not like that, and was open to giving the First Assembly of Sinai a second chance. There was a price, however, that Moses had to pay so he wouldn't forget this outburst. He was sent to his room for a time out, even though he didn't start the mess. For the first set of stone tablets, God provided the stone and Moses didn't need to carry them up the mountain. On the second set, however, God as good as said, "You broke them. You break it, you can fix it. Get your own stone this time and then I will write on these for you. You better not break them the second time, however! I am watching you, so do what I tell you to do." Sort of sounds like some of the dialogue we have with our kids from time to time: "You break it, you fix it."

Now Moses has to have another face-to-face with God. I bet the second trip up the mountain was a lot longer than the first trip. No stress here! Walking into the equivalent of a volcano knowing that God is upset with him. He had no idea what was in store for him. Again the place is on fire, lots of smoke, the whole deal. He also had a bigger load to carry. For the first trip he didn't have to pack a load of stone. The second trip he had to pack these two heavy pieces of stone both up and down. Moses was no young buck, don't forget. If you have ever done any hiking, you know that packing rock doesn't make for an easy trip.

> [1] *"And the LORD said to Moses, 'Cut two tablets of stone like the first ones, and I will write on these tablets the words that were on the first tablets which you broke.* [2] *So be ready in the morning, and come up in the morning to Mount Sinai, and present yourself to Me there on the top of the mountain"* (Exodus 34:1-2 NKJV).

Do you think Moses felt under any pressure here? "Moses, this is God speaking. We have a meeting set for 7:00 a.m. tomorrow. Be there!" A lesson to be learned from mountain climbing: if we don't listen to God for the first trip up the mountain, then each successive trip becomes more difficult until we finally get it right and do it God's way. Most of us know the story from Sunday School days. Do we still teach this in Sunday School?

Another random thought that leads to a question: have you ever wondered why it only took three months to get from Egypt to Sinai to meet God, including crossing the Red Sea? This seems pretty good speed to me since they were walking with 1,200,000 people! So why did it take another forty years of wandering around to get across a small river, the Jordan River, to the Promised Land? Not only did it take 40 years for the second leg of the promise, but it also meant that most of the "old guys" who left Egypt were dead and missed the prize. Ever thought of that? How much better we would be if we just did things God's way and without complaining. Things wouldn't take so long! Many fewer trips back up the mountains packing a load of rock!

Fast-forward now forty years: finally the First Assembly of Sinai got it together. Finally it is time for the Church to move into their promise. It took three days of prayerful preparation and the

Church was on the move. Another miracle plan—this time for crossing the Jordan River. No matter what the obstacles appear to be, God always has a plan to complete the impossible. All the Church needs to do is to stop complaining. Stop looking for a better way. Be patient and do Church God's way.

> [14] *"So it was, when the people set out from their camp to cross over the Jordan, with the priests bearing the ark of the covenant before the people,* [15] *and as those who bore the ark came to the Jordan, and the feet of the priests who bore the ark dipped in the edge of the water (for the Jordan overflows all its banks during the whole time of harvest)...and all Israel crossed over on dry ground, until all the people had crossed completely over the Jordan"* (Joshua 3:14-17 NKJV).

Not only did they cross on dry land, but God actually waited until flood season before moving them across the river.

God has a pretty cool way of crossing bodies of water. No waiting for the bridge to be built, or the ferry line-ups to pass or the floods to subside. Just walk across on dry land. Perhaps we should just get back to basics, and try walking across the challenges of Church "on dry land" and do it God's way for a change. The Ark—the Spirit of God—in the front and those of the Church following. Just as the scripture says, *"Do not come near it, that you may know the way by which you must go, for you have not passed this way before"* (Joshua 3:4 NKJV). We have never done it this way before is an expression we often hear. We should learn to try it sometime.

Many of the discussions and replies that I had while seeking an answer to my question seemed to come around to getting back to the early Church. The respondents had a wide variance in ideas as to what this looked like. Small groups, no organization, no leaders, home groups, meeting from house to house, and the list grew from there. Much of their answers seemed to focus on structure rather than relationship with Jesus.

Let's get back to the First Assembly of Sinai. It had a membership of 1,200,000 and yet it still functioned. How did they administer this whole thing? Moses must have been on the verge of burnout and run ragged continuously. The plan wasn't to reduce the group size but the plan was to have some help and organization.

An interesting sidebar to this instruction is that the wise council came from the father-in-law of Moses. Not all instruction needs to come with fire, smoke, and trumpets on a burning mountaintop. Wise people are available within the Church to assist us to get back to the basics. Can we just learn to listen? This passage is one of those instances of wise council. Why do we see examples of frustration and burnout in our present Churches, even though all Churches are small by comparison to the First Assembly of Sinai? A lack of listening to wise, Spirit-filled counsel.

> [13] *And so it was, on the next day, that Moses sat to judge the people; and the people stood before Moses from morning until evening.* [14] *So when Moses' father-in-law saw all that he did for the people, he said, 'What is this thing that you are doing for the people? Why do you alone sit, and all the people stand before you from morning until evening?'* [15] *And Moses said to his father-in-law, 'Because the people come to me to inquire of God.* [16] *When they have a difficulty, they come to me, and I judge between one and another; and I make known the statutes of God and His laws'"* (Exodus 18:13-16 NKJV).

Moses thought that he was the only guy that could minister to the Church. How about our modern Church pastors? Why not get some trusted help?

"So Moses' father-in-law said to him, "The thing that you do is not good. [18] *Both you and these people who are with you will surely wear yourselves out. For this thing is too much for you; you are not able to perform it by yourself.* [19] *Listen now to my voice; I will give you counsel, and God will be with you: Stand before God for the people, so that you may bring the difficulties to God.* [20] *And you shall teach them the statutes and the laws, and show them the way in which they must walk and the work they must do"'* (Exodus 18:17-20 NKJV).

Hey Moses! Teach the people the Word of God so that they can find the solution to most of their problems themselves from the Word of God. Sounds like a smart idea.

[21] *"Moreover you shall select from all the people able men, such as fear God, men of truth, hating covetousness; and place such over them to be rulers of thousands, rulers of hundreds, rulers of fifties, and rulers of tens.* [22] *And let them judge the people at all times. Then it will be that every great matter they shall bring to you, but every small matter they themselves shall judge. So it will be easier for you, for they will bear the burden with you.* [23] *If you do this thing, and God so commands you, then you will be able to endure, and all this people will also go to their place in peace."* [24] *So Moses heeded the voice of his father-in-law and did all that he had said"'* (Exodus 18:21-24 NKJV).

A following chapter will speak to this plan as well for the current day Church. The running of a vineyard demonstrates this structure well. Remember this chapter when you are reading the vineyard chapter. See if it has some similarities in answering the challenges of the burnout factor and the long lines at Sinai First Assembly.

Was the size of the Church a factor for Moses and Joshua and the children of Israel? The same question applies for any congregation, large or small. It is not the size of your Church body. The attitudes of the people and the inability to move as God instructed was the issue. They had heart issues and not size issues. There is no point in looking for some new system, or a new organizational chart, or some new chapter in some book that will define the perfect Church size. This truth applies to every member of the body from the head to its toe. The heart and the attitudes—with the focus on Jesus as their datum—is the key.

———

Okay, let's run the hypothetical question by one last time—this time with answers: "What if God came to you this morning, and spoke face to face and audibly to you. He says to you, 'I have chosen to grant you one wish. Think on this carefully. I will move you and the Church to any point in time that you request. Both you and the "normal" Church will be restored to the "normal" spiritual condition that my people are enjoying at that time.'"

A Summary in the actual words from your replies

(The names have been removed for privacy. Some of you reading this may recognize your comments.) The posted comments are arranged in the order that I received the replies from the respondents.

The Perfect Church # 1

What I took away from last night's discussion: After a quick overview of the Churches, I discovered that in five of the seven Churches there was *sin in the camp*.

- An examination in the camp of my heart is in order
- An examination of my local Church is in order

- An examination of the trends and direction of the national Church, universal Church is in order. I refer to evangelical, biblically-professing Church. I guess…
- These examinations should be in the light of the Word of God and not comparing to anything else.
- Jesus said that "without me you can do nothing." "The spirit is willing but the flesh is weak." All the above can only happen by the power of the Holy Spirit. We need to pray for an intervention, a revival, a Holy Ghost move, and not interfere with Him.

About the other thing, offhand, I would say that I wouldn't mind living in the 1950s Church, North America, because the nations had just come through the horror of WW2 and had been humbled, society supported Biblical principles, there were many evangelists reaching the lost for Christ (Billy Graham, etc.). Simple living.

The Perfect Church # 2

I would choose this time. For our Church I would pick the 90s revival time and hope that it would stay on course and not follow down rabbit trails, and keep the vision true. As far as a period in history it would be now as I feel we have more information and access to worship and the Holy Spirit is there as much as He was at the start.

I prayed to God all my life but never understood a relationship with Christ till my son brought me to Jesus and I went to a cell group. I came to Jesus in the late 90s.

The Perfect Church # 3

Great assignment! It let me spend a brief moment "tripping down memory lane" in Church history. I want to honour the request for a reply but will admit to not having an extended period to ponder as I might want...that having been said...I would request to move myself and the Church to its first and second century beginnings for the following reasons:

(a) eyewitnesses to the life and teachings of Jesus and the apostles were still alive and written eyewitness accounts existed to rely on

(b) there was an dramatic and obvious difference between those followers of THE WAY (Jesus) and those who did not

(c) although I have no masochistic tendencies, persecution of the followers of Jesus by both the Jewish hierarchy and Roman authorities produced anything but a "lukewarm" faith and only "sold-out" disciples of Jesus were seeking to live out their faith

(d) it was possibly relatively easy to initiate a conversation about GOD, the gods, spiritual matters at a time when the Jews were "looking" for the Messiah and "heathen" observed a pantheon of gods...Paul took advantage of this on Mars Hill in Act 17:22ff

(e) there was no media to blur, confuse, twist, or trump the message

(f) given that Jesus could have intersected human "time and space" history at any point along the continuum, and HE chose ~4-2 BC through ~ AD 30, I'll take it as a given that that period of history was most ideal to achieve HIS plan and purposes in launching HIS Church

---

The Perfect Church # 4

Wow! I immediately focus on 1980s. Many couples arrived at a new Church, the excitement of growth with good teaching. Many were excited about drawing closer to Christ and were anxious to share their faith. The new choruses were taken right out of scripture and covered all doctrine.

Personally, I was involved in teaching, leading men's fellowship, singles ministry. Our home had 31 singles for a weekly Bible study. My wife led women's ministry. I suppose our focus was totally on serving Christ. We were too busy to be self-absorbed. Most of my friends reflect on the close friends they had through growth groups in their Church.

The Perfect Church # 5

First Church and to be part of the Church as noted in Acts 1. Would be exciting to be a part of the first experience with the Holy Spirit, to see the start of the Christian Church from the ground up.

The Perfect Church # 6

Grant–Re: your question about where in Church History I would like to be – I want to be in Revelation Chapter 19 – verses 1-17

The Perfect Church # 7

That is a difficult question, though my 1st reaction would be to when the Holy Spirit first descended in Acts, after thinking about it, I'd like to be right here and in the now. This is where I'd like to be as people have and are learning from the good, bad, and ugly of the past. Though it seems like a slow process I know that God is at work and will do as He said he would do!!! Our past is not defined by what we did either right or wrong but by how we, and each future generation, are learning from it. This was a quick thought but what do you guys think about it???

The Perfect Church # 8

Thanks for sharing this. I do believe this is a truth on how we as Christians should see the Church and live. Believers defined not by what denomination, and loved through differences, and working for one purpose which is for His will (loving each other being a reflection of Him) and His kingdom purposes here on earth. Forgiving each other and when we do sin, lifting the other up and not condemning or judging. I do see a difference as you said on how some believers have come together in unity. What I am thinking is the perfection of this where all believers are in perfect and full unity, due to sin, will not happen until we are in heaven, but your writing this can spur on Christians to do as Christ would do!!! Thanks, as this is a great word and my prayer right now is for a revelation of this to believers!!!

The Perfect Church # 9

To a new point in time when people loved one another as much as Christ loved His Church.

Yes, I guess what interests me is the early Church as it set the foundation for the universal Church. When Christ said, "I will build my Church" (Matthew 16:18), I believe He meant His universal Church – first the Jews, proselytes, then Gentiles – all Christians everywhere. According to The Interactive Bible, the first Church was established in Jerusalem on the first Pentecost following Jesus' ascension.

One of the strengths of the first Church was brotherly love and unity (Acts 2:43-46; 4:32-37). All believers were "one in heart and mind" (referring to the sharing of possessions in this practical example). "May God give you the spirit of unity among yourselves as you follow Christ Jesus so that with one heart and mouth you may glorify God the Father..." (Romans 15:5-6). I believe that the first Church is the example for how we should live our lives today. The New Testament Commandment (which replaced the Old Testament's Ten Commandments) sums it up: Jesus said: "The most important one (commandment) is love the Lord your God with all your heart and with all your soul and with all your mind and with all your strength. The second is this: Love your neighbor as yourself. There is no commandment greater than these." (Matthew 22:37-40).

(An aside thought) During the Reformation it was believed that the Roman Catholic Church was the antichrist. (There have since been many other antichrists named by other religions.) However, we now know that there are many "born again" Christians who are Catholic. I am married to one, for example and know many, many others.

I believe, as the early Christians did, that the spirit of unity and loving God and your neighbor is the foundation of the Christian Church and should be the foundation of each individual's walk with Christ. That is why I believe it is for here on earth; not just in heaven. The early Church is our example.

The Perfect Church # 10

In my opinion, this is an ambiguous question. I don't believe that God would speak audibly face-to-face to us today. He speaks through his Word, i.e.: "Faith comes by hearing and hearing by the Word of God" (Romans 10:17).

Having said that, and I was to make a synopsis of this question, I would have to say that there is no time at all in history where there has been a normal Church. History has over and over shown an imperfect Church. Christ is coming for his perfect bride in the future - a bride without spot or wrinkle. This is the place (in the future not in history) where the most normal healthy spiritual condition of the Church will exist on this earth. The ultimate perfection will be when we have already been taken away and are enjoying the presence of the Lord for all eternity. "That He might present her to Himself a glorious church, not having spot or wrinkle or any such thing, but that she should be holy and without blemish" (Ephesians 5:27).

The road to being holy and without blemish is not easy, as the Church will face a falling away, deception, a time of persecution and testing, which is nothing new on this earth as the Church has seen that over and over. Even today many suffer and are persecuted. We need to look forward and not back to what the Lord has in store for those who love him. "But it is written: 'Eye has not seen, nor ear heard, nor have entered into the heart of man the things which God has prepared for those who love Him'" (1 Corinthians 2:9 NKJV).

The Perfect Church # 11

The year 1906. I think it would be 1906 (Azusa Street revival era).

The Perfect Church # 12

Hey, Grant: If God allowed myself and the Church to go back in time to anytime in church History I would choose the Welsh Revival led by Evan Roberts!! Through that Revival all of Wales was transformed!!! Bars became Churches, pub songs became worship songs, drunks became men of God, and countless miracles occurred!! There was true transformation!! Wales became 'Christian' and people began to fear the Lord and obey the Word. That would have been a great time for the Church, seeing souls saved and God's power at work.

The Perfect Church # 13

Very interesting question. I have thought about this for a few days. There are a couple of points but really I have to say the point I would want to go to is during the days of the early church…they seemed to be living in such harmony and no judgments. Since that time, it seems like the church has always been "in battle" to change, to get the message across or trying to make other denominations change. I liked that they were sharing everything and that everyone was taken care of and had what they needed.

HOWEVER, we wouldn't be transported in time would we because then I would have to ask for some indoor plumbing as well. Hee Hee hee.

Thanks for making me think about this. It was fun. Have a great day.

The Perfect Church # 14

Black Board Notes of a group of 20 ladies at their Wednesday morning Bible study. They reflected on the question and came to these findings. The leader asked the question and then wrote these points on the board as the ladies had them revealed to their hearts.

- ✓ Our relationship with Jesus is not fixed on a time or place in history or in the future. The time and place is found in our hearts and our attitudes and reverence towards the Holy Spirit.

- ✓ It is not a place in time but a space in time when our hearts are in tune with God. The most common space in time generally came back to the point when they accepted Jesus as their Savior and decided to follow Jesus. Their dates of salvation were at various dates in the past but the significance of their attitudes towards Jesus is the key.
- ✓ It is a time when their hearts were in the right place.
- ✓ Relationship with Jesus and with other Christians is of importance. Having communion with Jesus and with other believers that are in a healthy relationship with Jesus.
- ✓ A time when they are at the right place with God. This right place is not dependant on the Church but on the time that they spend with Jesus in prayer and in his Word.
- ✓ It is a time when they regain what has been left out and what has been lost. This is a time asking repentance for sin and repenting of allowing their hearts to grow cold.
- ✓ The place is the location of their hearts in relationship to the presence of Jesus. A time to stay away from murmuring, complaining, and tearing down others.
- ✓ A time when they have found their first love that has been lost. Again this comes back to repentance and a sorrow for sin that is insulating us from the presence of God.

The Perfect Church # 15

I think a good time for us was in 98/99 when we opened ourselves up before the Lord and viewed many others doing the same. The Church (*my home Church*) felt inclusive at that time and also felt victorious that Christ was on the throne and was alive and was a real and active PERSONAL Savior.

For me the whole Church experience has left me lacking at times and that's when the real dependency on Christ as my Personal Savior and I mean personal. No church can fill the need for a solid relationship with our Lord. Church is just a building we meet in for the fellowship, support, encouragement, and to feel free to praise our God. You can measure a church's health as to how it responds when going through a serious health concern or tragedy. You do learn and come to realize that we are not all spiritual islands. I have come to realize that the Gospel of Christ is the only constant. The words of an "old hymn" come to mind, The Church's one foundation is Jesus Christ her Lord. When we deviate it scares me, not for me but for the generations to follow. We have to meet to discuss this further. Thanks for making all of us THINK!

The Perfect Church # 16

Grant, sorry for the late reply. I would have to say the first five years after the day of Pentecost – so basically what the Church looked like in the first five chapters of the book of Acts as they say this scripture documents about five years of early Church history. I don't think we have gotten even close to reclaiming that ground yet.

After reading the above sample of replies from a wide spectrum of people, it is very obvious that we do not see a common date, past or future, for the perfect Church. We do not see a common structure for the perfect Church. Now that you have read the sample replies and have formed your own thoughts, answer the question for yourself. You will probably conclude that the perfect Church starts with you. I am sure that those from the head to the toes of the body will be reading this. The start of the perfect Church starts with your heart.

An interesting side note regarding some of the replies and those who did not reply other than with a correction. I had a couple of notes that did not express a period in time either past, present, or future to find the perfect Church. They offered me correction on my improper doctrine. I'm apparently not spiritual enough to understand that God does not grant wishes. He only answers prayers as long as they are according to his will. Also, now that we have scripture God no longer speaks to individuals other than through his Word. If I would get this fact right then I may be able to join their perfect Church.

Even sadder than this are the people who replied that they couldn't think of any time when God was really close to them. Not only could they not think of some special point in history or the future, but they could not think of a special time in their personal walk with God. Have we walked so long in God's freedom that we have become lost in it? Does a phrase come to mind: "I have lost my first love and now I am spiritually dead"? Could it be that some of us are drifting into dangerous water?

Oh, by the way, I also I had a comment on past revivals: "Not all Charismatics are the same, but that they all share the same guilt for their errors. Charismatics are the spawn of Pentecostalism. It is therefore prudent to see whether or not the child of Pentecostalism is just a wild and unprecedented mistake - or if it is a genealogical reproduction of its parent. If it is a mistake, then Pentecostalism might be exonerated. But, what if Charismaticism is a true child, an image of its parent? If this is so, then we have no option but to cast Pentecostalism into the same pit that Charismaticism belongs to."

Listening to this guy for sure will not help me find the Perfect Church. I now stand corrected. According to this guy, apparently the only denomination to have experienced an alleged false revival were the Pentecostals. At no point in this discussion have I mentioned denominations. This was an unsolicited reply to my posting, as I posted it on Facebook. I think I don't like his normal.

I had other replies that stated they found the question of interest but they could not think of any time period that would satisfy their needs. They failed to come up with any conclusion at all. They felt that a new location is more difficult to find than their current position.

After reading all of the replies it is interesting to note what is *not* being said. Nothing was said about the type or size of the organization. Not much was said about music and the style and type of worship. Nothing was said about the politics of the Church. Get my point? Much of the stuff that we read in books and are taught by the so-called wise guys does not seem to be all that important to those responding.

To one man, the best experience at Church was in the year that he met Jesus and became a Christian. This was his personal position defining "normal" for that year. To the "ladies study group" the common time boils down to the day they accepted Jesus as Savior. This is their personal position defining their ideal normal. Can you think of any time where you were closer to God than the day you received your adoption papers that made it official that you are a child of the King? The papers were signed by God making it official.

> [4] *"But when the fullness of the time had come, God sent forth His Son, born of a woman, born under the law, [5] to redeem those who were under the law, that we might receive the adoption as sons. [6] And because you are sons, God has sent forth the Spirit of His Son into your hearts, crying out, 'Abba,*

> *Father!'* [7] *Therefore you are no longer a slave but a son, and if a son, then an heir of God through Christ*" (Galatians 4:4-7 NKJV).

Some replies were in the future, such as in Revelation. This is a good point in time, but the unfortunate thing is I cannot get there until I am dead. Does this mean I am stuck in the sand until after death? Perhaps what they are seeing is a reference point to assist in a realignment of their hearts.

Perhaps we find many Exiting because they don't understand what Church is really meant to be. An even greater issue may be that our Churches don't understand what normal is to be. Do we see the same faults in our own spiritual lives that we saw in our challenged group of people that were part of Israel's First Assembly of Sinai? Think about all that Israel had in God with Moses as their leader, yet they missed the point.

Let's be careful next time we are complaining or attacking each other. Let's be careful lest we run off to follow some new system or organizational scheme and forget the real reason for Church. There is more to Church than just going back to some point in history and trusting that everything will be awesome. It is impossible to move backwards in time. Mistakes were made in the past and we can learn from these mistakes, so let's not fall into repeating the same errors over and over. All of us can only live in the present, so what are we going to do about our relationship today with God?

The other night I was listening to a testimony of a man from Turkey, Pastor Fikret Bocek. Fikret Bocek is familiar with the risk involved in professing one's faith in a Muslim land. According to the video. Shortly after his conversion in 1988, he was imprisoned and tortured for ten days when the country's Minister of Internal Affairs arrested all Protestant Christians. The story of his conversion from a Muslim to Christian is in itself amazing. What is even more amazing is his statement that the time he felt the closest to Jesus was during the ten days of torture. The torture was so gross and brutal that he was not willing to speak about it. To be free of the brutality all he had to do was say this simple phrase, "Allah is God and Mohamed is his prophet." He refused and endured the five days of punishment.

Not many of us would even think about our time of torture as the normal for our Christian walk. This has to be the greatest answer to the search for the best normal.

I think the nugget from this chapter will be the discovery that: **My normal is not based on a position in time but it is the condition of my heart.** To find the perfectly normal Church may be as simple as an alignment of my heart in relationship to Jesus. The journey may be as short as repentance.

> [4] *"Nevertheless I have this against you, that you have left your first love.* [5] *Remember therefore from where you have fallen; repent and do the first works, or else I will come to you quickly and remove your lampstand from its place—unless you repent"* (Revelation 2:4-5 NKJV).

(Go back to the love you had when you first believed.)

Well, with that thought in our mind, let's get out of the Old Testament. Perhaps we should look at the First Assembly of Acts for a time. I think it is time to start another chapter. Wow! This topic of EXITS is getting complex.

Now what would you answer if I was to ask this question again: "What is the place or space that you would find is the normal place that God wants you to be?"

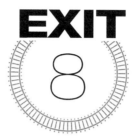

EXIT 8

FIRST CHURCH TO ABANDONED TRAINS

Our example of the First Assembly of Sinai, of course, is Old Testament, you say. How about the New Testament? The New Testament should be more relevant.

Let's review what was gained from the various thoughts of the previous chapter. This nugget may assist us to find normal.

My normal is not based on a position in time but it is the condition of my heart. To find the perfectly normal Church may be as simple as an alignment of my heart in relationship to Jesus. The journey may lead to repentance. The path is as short as back to the day that I accepted the invitation of Jesus to become a joint-heir of the king.

Perhaps the most frequently-chosen time period of the respondents was the first century Church and the Church of the book of Acts. But not much was said about what we are to look for in that time period, or what we are *not* to look for, as far as that goes. So now suppose you are standing Sunday morning in a Church described in the book of Acts. What would you experience if your heart was the same as it is at this precise moment that you are reading this chapter? A few touched on the fact that proper relationships with Jesus and fellow believers is important.

The book of Acts was written around AD 60. This is interesting because around the same time the activities recorded in Acts were taking place we have the issues as detailed in 1 and 2 Corinthians also taking place.

I am sure you have often heard it said that "if we could just get back to the first century Church then we would have the perfect Church." You are not alone as I have heard the same comments. Even more to the fact, and without much thought, I have said the same thing myself. I have read various books and heard a number of speakers all chanting the same mantra: "We need to get back to the early Church and the apostolic age" over and over. This is nothing more than a date in history unless we have a landmark that will show us that we are there. Rolling back the clock in some sort of time machine will do nothing. One reply did, in fact, nail it. I ALMOST FORGOT IT!

Here is the quote: "HOWEVER, we wouldn't be transported in time, would we, because then I would have to ask for some indoor plumbing as well. Hee Hee hee. Thanks for making me think about this. It was fun. Have a great day."

Simply moving back in time to the Acts Church will do nothing more than eliminate our nice toilets. Wow! That is profound, but true!

(Author's note: I am blessed to have found a great editor to help keep me on track and make sense. No small task, I am certain. Thanks, Ed! But this one I just can't resist. I need to break out of his grip once in a while. The following comment is from Ed.)

Chapter 8 - You say, "Simply moving back in time to the Acts Church will do nothing more than eliminate our nice toilets." Actually, as Internet articles say, "The Romans were one of the first known civilizations to invent indoor plumbing." And another article adds: "1st to 5th centuries AD: Flush toilets were used throughout the Roman Empire. With the fall of the Roman

Empire, the technology was lost in the West." So most middle-class Romans did have nice toilets. Mind you, the poor Jews of the early Church in Jerusalem probably did not have the benefit of Roman flush toilets and indoor plumbing, so maybe you can keep this statement and simply modify it.

My reply: "I think Ed has far too much time on his hands if he is researching ancient toilets."

Okay already! Enough about toilets. I am certain that the young lady who made the comment had no idea what she was unleashing.

To read some books you would think that the first century Church was the perfect Church. It makes the speaker sound all-knowing and really in touch. Just keep saying this phrase and all will be good. In our search, perhaps we should dig a bit deeper into this concept. We can learn something from every Church in the New Testament. We have the Bible as our manual.

We may have at least one New Testament Church that was close to being as perfect a Church as possible. The time period covered by Acts 1 to 5 appears to have kept a pretty pure focus. It is not until the account of Ananias, with Sapphira his wife, that we see any apparent wrong motives within the Church. They were caught up in pride and ultimately lied to the Holy Spirit. What a big price they paid for the sake of pride. This was not a long stretch in time, and we can only assume that after this account, other unrecorded selfish motives started to appear. Later in Acts 11 we see the Jews having issues because the Gentiles received salvation just like they had. We see a form of racism and pride cropping up. The Jews felt that salvation was exclusive to them and not the lowly Gentiles. Now we see the start of divisions as one group claims to be superior to another group. It was good while it lasted, but we mortals are a difficult bunch.

There are a number of first century Churches featured in the New Testament. For starters, go to the book Revelation. We have seven Churches detailed in this book. This is the first century with John recording his vision and writing the book in AD 95. Sounds pretty first century. But of the seven Churches detailed in Revelation, only two had the full approval of Jesus. For the remaining five we read this comment by Jesus, *"Nevertheless I have this against you…"* Jesus then goes on to point out the flaw that was evident in that particular Church. A pretty clear statement that all was not well in AD 95. It sure appears that they had many of the same issues that we are experiencing today. Could it have been their heart condition back then as well?

> [4] *"Nevertheless I have this against you, that you have left your first love.* [5] *Remember therefore from where you have fallen; repent and do the first works, or else I will come to you quickly and remove your lampstand from its place—unless you repent"* (Revelation 2:4-5 NKJV).

How about the first letter to the Corinthians, "The Troubled Church"? When was it written? Around AD 55, approximately 20-25 years after Jesus' death and resurrection. As you can see, it isn't enough to just grab a date from a calendar and then say they had it all together. There is more than just a date and place. Corinth had some big Church issues. Not a very good normal to try and pattern ourselves after!

They were a divided and infighting Church, so much so that Paul had to write them:

> [10] *"Now I plead with you, brethren, by the name of our Lord Jesus Christ, that you all speak the same thing, and that there be no divisions among you, but that you be perfectly joined together in the same mind and in the same judgment.* [11] *For it has been declared to me concerning you, my brethren, by those of Chloe's household, that there are contentions among you"* (*1* Corinthians 1:10-11 NKJV).

And they were a sexually immoral Church!

> [1] *"It is actually reported that there is sexual immorality among you, and such sexual immorality as is not even named among the Gentiles—that a man has his father's wife!* [2] *And you are puffed up, and have not rather mourned, that he who has done this deed might be taken away from among you"* (1 Corinthians 5:1-2 NKJV).

(What da yah think? Pretty gross stuff, hey? A man's son having sex with his step-mother. This meant his father also had more than one wife, other than the son's mother. The Church in Corinth, an early New Testament Church had issues of divisions and sexual immorality. Not a great normal to try and pattern ourselves after.)

One book that I read indicated that the whole key to success is to leave your current Church and form a small group Church. It went on to teach that the structure of the established Church is the problem. Just get together with a small group and have no structure but just come together from time to time and see what pops up. No leadership required. Just let people share what is on their hearts. No preparation needed. Just hang loose and see what comes up. Really? As far as I can see, this is just placing another Exit door in the body of Christ. Some that I know that have tried this plan are now sitting on a siding someplace. Worse yet, some are having troubles with their kids showing no interest in Church or the things of God. Can't imagine why?

Another word picture I would like you to visualize is this: like a train, Christians are traveling along on a track, not particularly fulfilled but at least in fellowship. Their Church can use some work, but it is better than no Church. Sad to say, but many seem to be in this space. We don't want to leave because we don't have any other destination Church in mind that is any different. Sort of just sticking it out with the best we have. Can't bring ourselves to leave because our circle of friends is here. Has a familiar ring to it. As uninspiring as this sounds, it at least beats the alternative.

Then one of these new philosophies comes along and encourages people to pull off the "main track" and pull onto a rail siding. The small group concept with "everything being common," no leaders, and no structure, has some appeal. The beauty of this is that the term consistent and regular is not part of the style. Just hang loose. Just keep singing "Free at last! Free at last! Thank God Almighty, we are free at last!" As they move along singing the refrain we hear their voices becoming more distant as they move away down the track. Once the shift has started it is so much easier to relax. Soon Church attendance becomes variable and they have less contact with other believers. They start to rust but continue saying that everything is good. The disgruntled then follow along on the siding track for a time but become less and less connected. Once on the siding they are then more exposed to the next fad for the perfect "New Testament" Church.

This makes it easier for them to start their Drift but they think they are good because, after all, they are part of a body. Once they become inconsistent and disconnected from the body then they can justify having a day off Church once in a while. Did I say once in a while? Hey, it's all good!

These fads are driven by a large range of theories.

✓ The size of the group should not be greater than 12 based on the fact that Jesus had 12 disciples. Small groups of 12 now head off on the next side track and languish there for a time.

✓ The next fad is that a small group is not structured and has no leadership. The teaching becomes spontaneous and turns a bit weird. Seen these as well. Another group of Christians is pulled off to another siding.

✓ If you have been around Church for a time you may recall the "Shepherding Movement" of the 1970s and early 1980s. Some great power trips evolved from this model. Some shepherds ended up with the wool from their sheep. Rich Shepherd = Broke Sheep.

✓ Numerous Churches have become "Seeker-friendly" Churches, disposing of the parts of the gospel message that might offend anyone's lifestyle. There is no hell, based on the idea that a loving God will not send anyone to hell. Another group now pulls off to a rail siding.

What do you think the next Christian Church fad will be? I am sure one is on its way down the track to seduce a few more onto the next rail siding.

As you travel around the country you may have noticed the presence of derelict and apparently abandoned rail cars sitting on some faraway track siding. A length of train cars is sitting in the Fraser Canyon in B.C. in exactly this setting. You can see the cars from the Trans-Canada Highway. I have been passing these forgotten rail cars for years as I travel north to go hunting. The cars are all rusting out, and the blackberry bushes are overgrowing the cars. It looks like the CNR railway has forgotten and abandoned these once-useful rail cars. They are on a track directly beside the main track. All day productive trains pass by on the main track. These sidetracked cars, however, just sit and rust! What a sad image!

NO LONGER USEFUL

(Do a google search for "**derelict rail cars**" and view some pictures. Think of the opportunity. You and your friends are free, and this could be you. Has anyone seen the kids lately?)

These cars are right alongside the main track but have been directed to various sidings, and then forgotten. A sad sight to view! This reminds me of the many forgotten Christians who have been lured to chase after these newfound schemes until they have become fully marooned and separated from the body. Of even greater tragedy is the fallout and damage caused by these well-meaning Christians pulling onto a rail siding. Those whom they drag with them suffer real damage. Have you thought about what effect this has on their kids, for instance? Many kids join their parents on the "Siding Church" and then just drift away. Bewildered parents and grandparents then wonder why they can't get their kids interested in Church. They have become abandoned just like those rail cars.

Over the years I have had some say to me that they are finding that now they are getting on in years they experience less temptation in their Christian walk. On more careful examination, the situation turns out to be that the devil no longer needs to tempt them and draw them away as they are already away and no threat to him. They have withdrawn from the Church and have settled on a rail siding in the bush some place, rusting away. What does the devil have to worry about with Christians who are parked on a siding? The devil knows enough to focus his energy on those who can cause him some damage.

So what are we looking for in our search? In our previous chapter we came to the conclusion that finding the ideal Church is as simple as having a right condition of our hearts. What we are *not* looking for then is:

- ☒ Another structure or system, or lack of structure.
- ☒ A different form or style with only a great music program.
- ☒ A shorter service or a longer service.
- ☒ Watered-down preaching to attract the numbers but without the need for repentance.
- ☒ A Church that is focused on growth rather than health.
- ☒ Little teaching for the Christians with a focus to the non-believer. Starve the Christians to seek the lost.
- ☒ I am sure you can add to this list. In fact, the list is endless, so what is the point of detailing them all?

Perhaps we should pull out the manual and see what the scripture tells us a New Testament Church should look like. I think that in the end this is what every Christian should be looking for in Church. Note that this scripture is directed to the Christians who are *in* the Church, and not to the nonbeliever that is outside of the Church. In essence, the Church is for believers and the New Testament describes how they are to interact with each other. The Church is not a factory for producing new Christians. Those seeking Jesus will be attending church and an opportunity should always be available for them to find him. There's a need for altar calls in our meetings, true, but for the most part, growth and evangelism is achieved with the focus on keeping the Christians healthy so that they can go outside of the Church and spread the gospel.

OPERATOR'S MANUAL FOR THE PERFECT CHURCH

We are to be one body with the purpose of supporting each other:

"I, therefore, the prisoner of the Lord, beseech you to walk worthy of the calling with which you were called, with all lowliness and gentleness, with longsuffering, bearing with one another in love, endeavoring to keep the unity of the Spirit in the bond of peace. There is one body and one Spirit, just as you were called in one hope of your calling; one Lord, one faith, one baptism;

We have one God and everything in the Church is to be honoring to God for the purpose of spiritual health.

"...one God and Father of all, who is above all, and through all, and in you all. But to each one of us grace was given according to the measure of Christ's gift. Therefore He says: 'When He ascended on high, He led captivity captive, and gave gifts to men.' (Now this, "He ascended"—what does it mean but that He also first descended into the lower parts of the earth? He who descended is also the One who ascended far above all the heavens, that He might fill all things.)

God has placed various ministries within the normal Church for the purpose of equipping the saints to be productive Christians.

"And He Himself gave some to be apostles, some prophets, some evangelists, and some pastors and teachers, for the equipping of the saints for the work of ministry, for the edifying of the body of Christ, till we all come to the unity of the faith and of the knowledge of the Son of God, to a perfect man, to the measure of the stature of the fullness of Christ;

Christians are to stop acting like children and understand that adults do not keep chasing the wind.

"…that we should no longer be children, tossed to and fro and carried about with every wind of doctrine, by the trickery of men, in the cunning craftiness of deceitful plotting, but, speaking the truth in love, may grow up in all things into Him who is the head—Christ—

The Church is a living body. Cultivate the various parts to grow together.

"…from whom the whole body, joined and knit together by what every joint supplies, according to the effective working by which every part does its share, causes growth of the body for the edifying of itself in love.

Understand that every new doctrine or the newest and greatest health drink may not be good for us. Beware genetically modified interpretations of scripture to advance some new point of view.

"This I say, therefore, and testify in the Lord, that you should no longer walk as the rest of the Gentiles walk, in the futility of their mind, having their understanding darkened, being alienated from the life of God, because of the ignorance that is in them, because of the blindness of their heart; who, being past feeling, have given themselves over to lewdness, to work all uncleanness with greediness. But you have not so learned Christ, if indeed you have heard Him and have been taught by Him, as the truth is in Jesus:

Certain conduct and activity is to be avoided. Don't allow the margins to become fuzzy. This can only be prevented by teaching and a desire to change. "Repentance" may be the key word here.

"...that you put off, concerning your former conduct, the old man which grows corrupt according to the deceitful lusts, and be renewed in the spirit of your mind, and that you put on the new man which was created according to God, in true righteousness and holiness. Therefore, putting away lying, "Let each one of you speak truth with his neighbor," for we are members of one another. "Be angry, and do not sin": do not let the sun go down on your wrath, nor give place to the devil. Let him who stole steal no longer, but rather let him labor, working with his hands what is good, that he may have something to give him who has need.

Speak as one who is a true child of the King. (Listening to people's speech can give us good insight into their culture and upbringing. We normally only listen for a few seconds before we form opinions as to their status in life: "A bit rough around the edges and poorly-educated," or, "Highly-refined or wise person." You can even tell if some are from afar by listening to their speech. You can even tell their country of origin.)

"Let no corrupt word proceed out of your mouth, but what is good for necessary edification, that it may impart grace to the hearers. And do not grieve the Holy Spirit of God, by whom you were sealed for the day of redemption.

We have a code of conduct between Christians. Relationship is key in a healthy and normal Church.

"Let all bitterness, wrath, anger, clamor, and evil speaking be put away from you, with all malice. And be kind to one another, tenderhearted, forgiving one another, just as God in Christ forgave you."

(Courtesy of the Apostle Paul in Ephesians 4:1-32 (NKJV), AD 61, during his first Roman imprisonment.)

We cannot go back in time. We are stuck with the present, indoor plumbing and all. But we can pick up on some of the important points from the past and implement them into our plan for the perfect Church.

A few points of note from the Acts of the Apostles: the Christians were compelled to gather together in a spirit of unity and continue to pray until the Holy Spirit arrived.

"These all continued with one accord in prayer and supplication" (Acts 1:14 NKJV). There was a common focus and unity of the group to see what God had for them.

It was of prime importance to have a structure that was according to the original plan as laid out by Jesus. Eleven wasn't good enough for leadership, it was important to get back to the original plan of 12 apostles. God really nitpicks on details.

"And they cast their lots, and the lot fell on Matthias. And he was numbered with the eleven apostles" (Acts 1:26 NKJV). The group was not a random group without structure. It was important that they returned to the leadership of 12 as Jesus had originally formed. Judas, of course, was gone, and it was important to bring the number of the leadership group back to 12.

The myth that only small groups will work. Do the math. An important fact should not be lost here. No matter what size of group gets together—large or small—it will fail if the motives are wrong and the hearts are in the wrong place. Size is not the key. Any size will do depending on the conditions. Some areas have few Christians. Church, of course, will be a small group. Other Churches may be larger. You be the doctor and get out the stethoscope. We must check the heart condition of the man in the mirror.

Acts 1:15 (NKJV) says that *"altogether the number of names was about a hundred and twenty."* The group meeting together was not a small group. There were women present also and they were not counted as was the Jewish custom of that day. This practice is detailed in Acts 4:4 (NKJV) which says that *"the number of the men came to be about five thousand."* The women were not counted. The meeting could have been much larger than 120. So much for "Only small groups need apply."

At a recent census the average people population (the "mean") of a given local Church in North America is 184 people. Or you might come at it from the perspective that this means that half of the Churches in America have 75 people or less (the "median"). This Church in Jerusalem was a full Church that was waiting in one accord.

This small group was gaining in size so quickly that they needed help to manage the growth. Enter Deacons. These were not just some ordinary Joes who needed recognition. They were full of the Holy Spirit and had the health and spiritual welfare of the Christians at heart.

"…seek out from among you seven men of good reputation, full of the Holy Spirit and wisdom, whom we may appoint over this business" (Acts 6:3 NKJV). The organizational structure comes together. The Random Small Group concept was quickly expanding. The "small group" was gaining strength and now we have the need to look after the widows or the business of the Church. We now have deacons in the mix—seven of them who are full of the Holy Ghost. Only small groups will work, some say? Looks like this Church quickly blew past Small Group.

Enter the cash. Did we have high-pressure teaching on giving? Nope!

32 "Now the multitude of those who believed were of one heart and one soul…34 Nor was there anyone among them who lacked;

for all who were possessors of lands or houses sold them, and brought the proceeds of the things that were sold" (Acts 4:32, 34 NKJV). We don't see any great pressure to raise money. When the Holy Spirit touches hearts the generosity follows. Do you see any high-pressure teaching on tithing in Acts? No, but the money is there. This didn't give an excuse for the Christians to *not* give, but their hearts felt compelled to give. They didn't appear to have freeloaders as a problem. Their hearts were right and they wanted to give.

The teaching on money seemed to be at odds with the Old Testament tithing concept.

4 *"While it remained, was it not your own? And after it was sold, was it not in your own control?"* (Acts 5:4 NKJV). This is much different from some of our current teaching. In some modern meetings, as much time is spent wringing money out of people as in the message. The apostle Peter is telling all present that the finances of the individuals were their own and there was no pressure for them to give. Paul repeats this "no compulsion" theme in 2 Corinthians 9:7.

Already the problems pop up with this new freedom. Enter the spirit of pride and the need of those with money to put on a show. *"'You have not lied to men but to God.'* 5 *"Then Ananias, hearing these words, fell down and breathed his last"* (Acts 5:4-5 NKJV).

Now the youth group in this new Church had a new task. The young men were in charge of body removal from those cheating on their offering (Acts 5:6). Don't jump to conclusions with this! They were not dead for holding back. They didn't need to give anything. They were dead for hypocrisy, pride, and lying. The money was theirs to keep if they so wished and no pressure for doing so…other than their pride.

The true doctrine from the book of Acts will stand the test of time.

"And now I say to you, keep away from these men and let them alone; for if this plan or this work is of men, it will come to nothing; [39] *but if it is of God, you cannot overthrow it—lest you even be found to fight against God"* (Acts 5:33-40 NKJV). Some very wise counsel. Look at the test of time to see if a New Fad Theology will work or not. If it is false it will fail and if it is true it will endure. Has the real story in the book of Acts endured? Yes. How about the fiction about the book of Acts? No. The new modified plans have all failed. But the truth in the New Testament Church has endured.

EXIT 9

THE VINEYARD

I LOVE VISITING VINEYARDS. IF YOU HAVEN'T DONE A WINERY TOUR and a tour of their vineyards, then I think you may have trouble understanding John 15. It may sound like I am trying to book tours and lead you into trouble by encouraging you to drink grape juice. Not so.

You may think I am joking, but this time I am stating a fact. I have actually had comments made to me such as, "We don't want to support something that is opposed to scripture and participate in something that is against the Church." Others have said that they don't wish to do a winery tour because they are afraid of what their Christian friends may think and they don't want to cause any to stumble. Am I making this stuff up? I had this exact conversation at various times with a pastor of a Church that I attended and on another occasion with an evangelist I know. That went over big!

If you have been around Church for a while, I am sure you have a list of reasons that would keep you from doing research on John 15. If, in the end, you are still reluctant to take a field trip then tell them (your critics) that your pastor told you to take the trip. That should make it all good. On a more serious note, however, you do not need to drink anything but water. The best time of year to go on a tour is about August and it is usually hot.

In the Okanogan region of B.C. are some large vineyards. Another area of particular fame, of course, is the Tuscany area of Italy. My wife and I have had the experience of staying for about a week in a vineyard in both of these areas. If you want to experience the real deal, you can book accommodation, swim in the pools, eat at nice restaurants, and spend time touring the vineyards and view the complete winery process. We did this experience only for educational reasons, however, and found it very relaxing and informative. This experience will not only "strike the original match" with your wife, but it will give a whole new perspective on John 15.

> [1] *"I am the true vine, and My Father is the vinedresser.* [2]*Every*
> *branch in Me that does not bear fruit He takes away; and*
> *every branch that bears fruit He prunes, that it may bear*
> *more fruit.* [3]*You are already clean because of the word which I*
> *have spoken to you.* [4]*Abide in Me, and I in you. As the branch*
> *cannot bear fruit of itself, unless it abides in the vine, neither*
> *can you, unless you abide in Me.* [5]*"I am the vine, you are the*
> *branches. He who abides in Me, and I in him, bears much*
> *fruit; for without Me you can do nothing.* [6]*If anyone does not*
> *abide in Me, he is cast out as a branch and is withered; and*
> *they gather them and throw them into the fire, and they are*
> *burned.* [7]*If you abide in Me, and My words abide in you, you*
> *will ask what you desire, and it shall be done for you.* [8]*By this*
> *My Father is glorified, that you bear much fruit; so you will*
> *be My disciples.* [9]*"As the Father loved Me, I also have loved*
> *you; abide in My love.* [10]*If you keep My commandments,*
> *you will abide in My love, just as I have kept My Father's*
> *commandments and abide in His love.* [11]*"These things I have*

spoken to you, that My joy may remain in you, and that your joy may be full" (John 15:1-11 NKJV).

John 15 is an exact quote from Jesus. What better instruction can I and the Church have if we wish to be fruitful? This may also give us a few pointers to determine what a normal Church may look like. A few points jump out at me after reading this passage:

1. Jesus is the vine.
2. God is the vinedresser (owner of the vineyard).
3. Pruning is required in order to produce fruit and have a productive vineyard.
4. You are already clean because you have God's Word.
5. You and I cannot bear fruit unless we are attached to the vine—Christ Jesus.
6. A branch that is not attached to the vine is of no value and will die.
7. If you are in Christ and have his Word in your heart "*you will ask what you desire, and it shall be done for you*" (verse 7).
8. Jesus gave us this promise "*that My joy may remain in you, and that your joy may be full*" (verse 11).

To start this topic off, let's look at the last point (8). *"That the joy of Jesus may remain in me, and that my joy in Jesus may be full."* Are most Christians experiencing this joy? Am I? If they are experiencing this joy, then are they experiencing this joy in their particular Church? Many are, but not all are. If they were experiencing this joy in their Church, then why are many standing in the Exits and why are many leaving? I think the answer is obvious: No, they are not experiencing this joy.

I heard from a recent survey that the Church is showing signs of decline. It is estimated that as many as two leave the organized

Church for every new believer that joins. One step forward and two steps backwards is not good. My personal belief is that unless some changes take place to the Church in North America, we will not recognize it in another 20 years. This should not come as a big shock. Just look at the evolution of the North American Church in the last 20 years. Topic for a different book.

When I recall most sermons I have heard on John 15, they are usually directed towards individuals (in the singular), and it is taught as if Jesus were only speaking to one person and his or her relationship to Christ. This is a valid interpretation, but not the whole picture. In my opinion it also relates to the Church body, both locally and universally.

In this passage it is pretty clear that Jesus is speaking to a group of people, his disciples whom he had trained and mentored. This was included in his final instructions to them after eating their final meal together, the Last Supper, just prior to the cross. Perhaps it was his final analogy or parable to emphasize a point of what their relationship to God would be and what their position in the Church (that was soon to be birthed) would be.

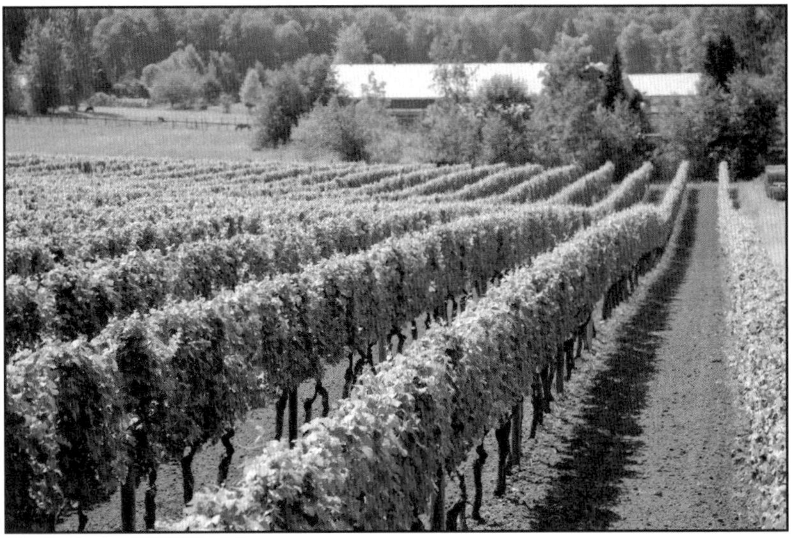

When I look outside of the box, I see a structure of not just one plant or vine, but of many plants that make up God's vineyard, the global Church. Each of the disciples would become a vineyard manager (pastor) attending to the cultivation of individual plants, that collectively will become individual Churches (the vineyard). The local Church may be one of many plants in the vineyard and be part of God's vineyard, the one Church of believers all over the world. The pastor may oversee the care of the particular branches, and is also an integral part of the vine but is not the owner.

Here's another true life story about something that I am doing with little (actually, poor) success. I am not good at growing grapes. You are gathering by now that I think grapes are cool. I decided that growing a little vineyard couldn't be all that difficult, so why not start my own? This will show you how dumb I am. I tried planting some grape seeds from grapes in the fridge. These eating grapes were amazing grapes, tasted great, and were huge. I think they were some special variety of grapes from Chile. I love eating these grapes!

Do you know that you can't grow grapes from seeds? Try planting grape seeds. You get nothing. Been there done that. I planted some seeds from these amazing grapes. After a long wait of staring at the pot of dirt…nothing.

I sent an email to the Botanical Department of UBC (the University of British Columbia) about my problems with planting grapes from seed. The first opening statement in their reply was a big clue to me. Quoted from their email: "Why would you want to try that?" They went on to say, "Grape seeds are not easy to germinate as they have a very high proportion of dormancy. I don't have actual figures, but I would guess that over 99% of grape propagation is by clonal methods (cuttings, grafting, and micropropagation)." I added to their research and proved to UBC that this was the case. Nothing happened. My seeds just laid there in a pot and did nothing until they eventually rotted.

To propagate the vines in the vineyards (Churches) you need to start with cuttings from a thriving, original, and productive plant. You do not start with a cutting from a non-productive and sick or dying plant.

So I go to the garden shops to buy six plants that were started from, I assume, good plant cuttings. I planted these and four died by the following year. The two remaining plants do give pretty good shade and a very small amount of fruit, but the birds ate all of the few grapes that they produced. I found out that it takes about two years after planting to produce enough fruit for a few birds to eat.

Back to UBC to find out what happened. Their reply to my email this time was: "Any well-drained soil with (hopefully) full sun, southern exposure will do. The variety depends on what you want out of your Grapevines: Wine? and what kind of wine—red or white? Table or eating grapes? Seeded or seedless? Or perhaps just shade and bird food?" I apparently chose the variety for shade and bird food. Still, I wondered: why would I choose to plant vines that produce seeded grapes if you can't grow grapes from seeds? Different topic.

Now they tell me. The soil is also important, I need to know what I am trying to produce with my grape vines, and if I can produce that in my particular area, and the exposure to the sun is important. Get my point with all of this. A healthy Church or vineyard just doesn't happen. Do any thoughts about our chapter on datum or the comments about a normal Church come to mind? We need to have some focus and direction as to where we are going with Church. What is our benchmark?

Pushing deeper into this thought, take a close look at the organizational structure of a successful and productive vineyard.

Every plant needs to be productive, and great care is given to the tending of each vine to make sure that fruit is produced. Why does a winery want to have a vineyard in the first place? They want it to produce lots of fruit, to make it profitable by producing excellent product. The passion of these vineyard owners is over the top. They do not just want good product, they want excellent product or fruit. This does not happen by accident.

Compare this with my little vineyard. Mine looks like a jungle experiment to produce a home for hungry birds. Not so in a well-tended vineyard where every act is performed with care to detail.

On your winery tour you will see that this is the case. The owner of the vineyard is very passionate about what he is doing. On your tour make sure that you try to meet and talk to the owner or the vineyard manager. These guys are enthusiastic about their vines, their fruit, and their product. They travel all over the world to wine competitions and have a display room set up for their awards. They are not doing all of this just because they like grapes.

Now take a look at the leadership structure of a successful winery. I removed the names from my sample, but the rest is copied from an actual company's profile. Read through this list. I think it will prove of interest as we work through the concept of the vines and the vineyard. In a few minutes it will hopefully make sense why I am including this.

Sample Winery

The OWNER started the vineyard in 1972 and remains as the current owner.

The Managing Director *provides leadership to the organization, and is directly responsible for winery contracts, financial, and legal matters, partner relations, and defining company goals, plans and strategies. Thirty-five years of* *management experience are equally balanced between consulting and operating management. His exposure to a wide variety of industries, markets, and technologies provides valuable insight to alternative strategies and methods.*

***The General Manager** oversees all the horticultural, marketing, and operations management skills acquired through running his own vineyard business for 30 years prior to joining us.*

***The Vineyard Manager** has a degree in Horticulture from _____ ____ University and continuing education in "Grapevine Anatomy & Physiology" and the "AgForestry Leadership Program." He came to us from _____ Wine Estates where he was a Viticulturist overseeing 2,500 acres of company and 1,500 acres of contracted vineyards. His technical training and palate for fine wine provide him the tools to translate winemakers' goals into vineyard practices.*

***Field operations** are supervised by two of the best in the industry. Staff (A) started with the Company in 1974, and has been the Production Manager for our winery since 1982. Staff (B) joined the Company in 1979, and has been the Production Manager since 1986. He received the prestigious "Grower of the Year Award" from the ______ Association of Wine Grape Growers. Together they have played key roles in developing the vineyards from infancy to where they are today.*

End of quotes from Sample Winery

Wow! This growing grapes stuff takes some dedicated and smart people with some expertise, knowledge, and passion. This is a lot more indepth than eating a few grapes, spitting the seeds into a flower pot, and trusting that it will produce more of the great grapes that I love to eat. Doesn't work. Even if you could get the seeds to germinate, other factors determine if they will be viable vines. Soil conditions of the new vineyard and the exposure to the sun are some examples. Seeds from grapes from Chile may not do well on my farm in Langley, B.C. Conditions are different, and even though we have some excellent award-winning vineyards in Langley, I am not the owner of one of them—as you may have guessed by now!

Sometimes I feel, however, that this is how many of our Churches are operating. We send out our spies to get the secrets from another Church, we read the current book on the most up-to-date programs for Church growth, then try to get some seeds from this particular model and plant them and see what happens, hoping also for a more successful Church plant. Yet in all this, the point of a team approach, education, and finding the mission of the Church is missed. Does the mission of the Church include a thought into the needs of the Christians who are attending? What are the soil conditions, and what are the geographical locations and the demographics and so forth?

Not every Church can be a copy of another vine that appears to be doing well because it has found its God-given mission for the particular body of Christians that make up the branches. Based on a number of elements—just as with grapes—various varieties are suited to certain needs and soil conditions. They are all from the vine of Jesus but different varieties are not uncommon.

Why do we have so many different denominations, for instance? Different denominations are just different varieties of the same vine. Certain core doctrines are not negotiable or subjective. These are referred to sometimes as "foundational truths" from scripture. The virgin birth, the Trinity, the deity of Christ, the Holy Spirit—these are foundational to being a Christian. Other areas can be discussed and debated, but not all Christians adhere to all of these non-foundational doctrines. You can still be a Christian (and *are* a Christian) even though we may not agree on all of these lesser points. I heard a joke onetime about six theologians gathered in a room: Confusion.

Even the styles of our services may differ from Church to Church. To listen to some people, however, you would think that they are the only way to go, and everyone else is missing the boat and are second-tier Christians. This sometimes comes up big-time, especially if a Church finds itself in the midst of a "refreshing" or, as some like to call it, a revival. Whatever your flavor and preference is, once the big ego kicks in, it is usually a sign that the next decline is not far off.

Some people like their worship to be calm, some like a more liturgical meeting, some like all the stops pulled out and just givin' it. If you want to get a real war going just bring up the topic of M-U-S-I-C. Actually, it *used* to be called music. Not any longer. It is now worship. In the end, however, what is the purpose of the Church?

The purpose of the Church is to worship God, study his Word, pray, love one another, support one another, help each other, partake of the Lord's Supper together, to learn how to live as godly people, and to be equipped to evangelize the world. The Church body is to collectively exhort us, to encourage us to become more like Christ, to guard the proper teachings of the Church, and to make sure that the believers don't drift off into some weird doctrines. I am sure that the list can be added to significantly.

Yet we so easily forget that these are the basic purposes of the Church. Do we even forget who the owner of the vineyard is? Don't overlook the fact that in our John 15 description of a healthy grape vine, Jesus makes it clear that even Jesus is not the owner, and yet many Christians act as if the Church is *their* property exclusively. Jesus makes it very clear that God his Father is the owner. Jesus is the vine. Jesus is the portion that is planted in the soil and contains the root and main stem that all of the various branches originate from. It is not the vine, however, that produces the fruit. The branches do—as long as they abide in the vine, that is.

Pruning is an important aspect of producing a healthy vineyard. We always like to push for growth in our Churches. Growth is good. I'm all for it, but healthy growth is what we need. Now that we have hit the topic of pruning as the third point, I would like to recommend an excellent book on this topic: *Necessary Endings* (Harper Business, January 10, 2011) by Dr. Henry Cloud. This is not a book about Church growth, but many of the concepts in the book will apply to building a healthy vine and branches. Dr. Cloud covers pruning very well in his second chapter, "Pruning: Growth Depends on Getting Rid of the Unwanted or the Superfluous." There are many memorable statements such as, "Your life produces more buds than you can nurture. Come to grips with the truth you can only nurture so many."

Hold on now. Be careful not to read into this comment something that I am not saying. The people always count, and people are what the Church is all about. The Church is an encouragement and support group assisting Christians to grow in their walk with the Lord. What about programs, however? Do we have an abundance of programs that seem good according to the Church growth manuals, but are not working for a particular Church body?

In Dr. Cloud's book he gives a good overview of pruning. When we talk about "necessary endings," it's important to understand the theory behind the three reasons for pruning. We need to prune if what we have is—

A) Good but not best

B) Sick and not getting well

C) Dead

It is one thing to understand this. It is quite another thing to apply these concepts in real life. In his book he is using the analogy of a rose bush. We are talking about grapes, but the same principle applies. When pruning a rose bush the first step is to ask, "What does a rose look like?" In other words, you have to know the standard you are pruning toward. This is not different than the manager of the vineyard—or the ideal Church. Do we know what the normal functioning Church looks like? Vineyard managers and successful business owners know the answer. Why is it so difficult for Churches to grasp this principle?

At the beginning of this chapter, point 4 states that we are already clean because we have God's Word. I take this to mean that the vine and the branches that are to produce fruit are already Christians. The Church is a body of believers that is planted to produce fruit. It sometimes appears that the Christians in a Church are secondary to non-Christians. Many churches are mainly geared towards the unbelievers as the Church attempts to fulfill the Great Commission. The sermons, the programs, and many of the efforts are directed towards the unbelievers and the believers are neglected.

You and I cannot bear fruit unless we are attached to the Vine—Christ Jesus. This isn't rocket science. Cut a branch off from the vine and it dries up and dies. This is my concern with the exit of believers from the Church. This fact is the reason I have this image in my mind at the start of this book. It is important for us to be connected to a healthy Church. An army of one will soon be defeated. Those exiting remain Christians but they will grow weak as they have no community of support to draw from. Without the support, encouragement, and teaching of the Church I will quickly become weak and unable to survive the attacks from the devil that are sure to come. Is this not the case with many that we know who have already exited the Church? How about the increased level of depression for example of Christians. Just a thought.

Now back to the example of our successful winery to see some pretty strong evidence that the wine business appears to have grasped some truths that the Church may want to pay attention to. Churches go through cycles as any organization does, but they seem to have more than their fair share of cycles. It has become evident that a young person choosing to go into ministry may find ministry to be an unsettling experience. More and more we hear about pastors leaving the ministry because of burnout and disappointment. I know a number of young people that have considered ministry as their vocation in life. After a few years they have made comments such as, "The church just chewed me up."

For this discussion, let's give the ***Founder*** of the vineyard the role of pastor. In the example of our successful winery, it is still owned by its founder of 34 years ago. In this time it has grown from a vineyard of about 100 acres to a much larger vineyard. I don't have the exact number, but it is now in the range of about 3,000 acres. Pretty good growth I would say, and he still has not reached the burnout stage.

For this discussion, let's give the ***Managing Director*** role to perhaps an assistant pastor—or in a smaller Church how about an elder with good common sense and spiritual experience. Just as with our vineyard, the founder still maintains his role of direction and energy and wisdom, but he does not feel threatened when seeking the advice and support of a person who may have a different skill set in certain areas, and shares the same goals as the founder. It is very clear that this person is most likely not a "yes guy" and has been seasoned with life experiences and skills. In our winery example, the Managing Director has been in business and a vineyard owner for at least 30 years prior to joining our sample winery.

For this discussion, let's give the ***Vineyard Manager*** role to the elders. The elders do not feel threatened by the pastor and should not be a threat to the pastor. They have the common goal to see the vineyard prosper and be full of healthy branches stemming from the vine of Jesus. We don't need to look very hard to find their qualifications. As a starter try a few scriptures such as: Elders lead the Church (1 Timothy 5:17; 1 Peter 5:1-2), teach and preach the Word (1 Timothy 3:2; Titus 1:9), protect the Church from false teachers (Acts 20:17, 28-31), exhort and admonish the saints in sound doctrine (1 Timothy 4:13; 2 Timothy 3:13-17; Titus 1:9), visit the sick and pray over them (James 5:14), and judge doctrinal issues.

For this discussion, let's give the ***Field operations*** role to the deacons. The deacons are not threatened by the pastor or the elders and should not appear to be a threat to the pastor. They have the common goal of wanting to see the vineyard prosper and be full of healthy branches stemming from the vine of Jesus. Just as in our winery example, you will find this is direct from scripture complete with the selection process and the qualifications. The term deacon appears at least 29 times in the New Testament.

The role or office of deacon was developed in the early Church primarily to minister to the physical needs of the members of the body of Christ. In Acts 6:1-6 we see the initial stage of development. After the outpouring of the Holy Spirit on Pentecost, the Church began to grow so fast that some believers, particularly widows, were being neglected in the daily distribution of food and alms.

So much for the myth that only small groups will work. As the Church expanded, logistical challenges arose at meetings simply because of the size of the fellowship. The apostles, who had their hands full caring for the spiritual needs of the Church, decided to appoint seven assistants who could tend to the physical and administrative needs within the body. Read Acts 6:2-4. Does this mean that the deacons only do the heavy lifting and have no part in ministry? Not so, but their roles may differ slightly. As proof, two of the seven deacons appointed here in Acts were Stephen (who later became the first Christian martyr) and Philip (who later became a leading evangelist). That sounds like they were in ministry. You may not prefer the role of martyr, however.

A notable point about a successful winery or vineyard is the stability of the organization. Read the bio of each of the participants in our sample vineyard. It starts with the founder who has remained since 1972. The rest of the participants are in the 30-year range. Not much turnover. Stability is a key thing. Does this mean that there is no room for the young guys? I am sure that you will find a few qualified young people working their way up the ranks to positions of importance within our sample organization. This will not happen, however, without experience.

The other day Cherril and I were sitting by the sea and watching its motion. The tide was starting to flood, the surf was rolling in, and the waves were breaking on a distant reef. A cool sight and very soothing to watch. I mentioned the reason that I find the sea so interesting is that it is in constant motion and change, and is like a living thing. The sea is never still. Sometimes I feel that the Church is more like the sea than a peaceful vineyard. It appears to be never settled and is in constant change and strife. Good for the sea! But not good for a vineyard.

A vineyard must be peaceful and settled, and work in fine order. Everything shows order and planning as the vines are all planted in rows. Every vine is an exact duplicate or reproduction of the neighboring vine. Ever wonder why you can't grow grapes from seeds? This is because each vine needs to be grown from a cutting of a producing vine. Every vine must be an exact duplicate of Jesus, the true vine in our illustration. Growth by planting cuttings would also be a great concept in the Church as well—every new vineyard an exact copy of Jesus. This would take the pressure off the need to mimic the most up-to-date Church growth book. This would be getting closer to the "normal Church" that we have been looking for.

Maturity with stability in a vineyard is good and leads to success. I mentioned earlier that we had a visit to Italy a few years ago and visited a few vineyards and wineries in Tuscany. One thing that I noted is that Italy is old. They don't tear anything down. As a real estate developer this is a concept that left me with some challenges. Even the house we were staying in was considered to be one of the newer homes in the area. It was 800 years old!

One particular vineyard and winery that we visited had been planted around AD 1160. They prided their fine wine as being produced from the same vines that were planted over 850 years ago. My first question of course was, "Does this mean that all of the vines we are looking at are over 850 years old?" The vineyard manager I was speaking to didn't know for sure as he wasn't that old. His answer was similar to this: (His Italian was great, but you had to listen carefully to understand his English.) "Most grape vines live for many, many years and some that are just planted will outlive you. Their fruit's quality will improve with each passing year. The older the vine, the better the wine."

How did they maintain the quality and make sure that the wine was consistent with the wine that they started producing in AD 1160? His reply was: "When a vine needs to be replaced because it is damaged or struck with disease, we will *only* replace it with a cutting from one of the best plants that is in the vineyard. Every vine in our vineyard is a direct descendant for the original vines from the original vineyard. This is why our wine is the *best wine in the world*."

Remember I started out stating that with these vineyard types, their passion for grapes is over the top? The young man we were talking to had a lifelong dream of being a wine master. He had gone to university for five years, worked in the vineyards tending the vines, and then as an assistant to the wine master of the winery. He was in his late thirties and had recently been appointed as Master Vintner for the winery. Does this answer the question about room to grow for the young guys? There is plenty of room for the young to move up to roles of leadership and authority. They do so, however, with education and careful direction under good mentors.

I think Cherril really liked this part of the tour. I recall some comment she made to my daughter, Lacey. "This young man is gorgeous" is the phrase that comes to mind. Lacey seemed to agree. Cherril kept referring to him as "the young man." Next time you see my wife or my daughter ask them about the Winery that we had lunch at in Tuscany and the "young man" who was giving us the tour. I found it hard to compete. My pride was shattered. I said that in the wine business, "old is good." According to Cherril and Lacey, in this case, young apparently looked pretty good too! Personally, I didn't see what all the fuss was about…nice guy, I guess.

I could go on and on about the amazing things I have learned about vineyards. I can also give you some up-to-date information about attempting a vineyard without paying attention to the details that are modeled by the master vineyard founders. Have a look sometime at my pathetic attempt at growing a few grapes to feed myself and a few lousy birds.

My problem is that I get distracted with work and other things. I don't really have the same passion that the owners of the wineries have about grapes. In the end, the results of my unorganized efforts are very evident. My grape "bushes" appear to have a similarity to some rare plant that is sprouting out of the jungles in the Amazon. Branches and sprouts everywhere, what a mess! Good shade though. After about five years of me attempting to produce some fruit, Cherril is still buying our grapes from the market.

Now this brings us to the statement that Jesus made as point (7) of our discussion at the beginning of this chapter. If you are in Christ and have his Word in your heart "*you will ask what you desire, and it shall be done for you.*"

I have to admit that this statement and others similar to it in the scriptures have caused me some difficulty over the years. I have heard lots of sermons on this, and have read various commentaries on this. It usually ends up with the feeling that God is sort of my "Genie in a bottle" and all I have to do is rub it like Aladdin's lamp and bam, I get what I want. Would be great but it doesn't work like that. I am sure you have found this to be true as well.

Not until I got a handle on a basic understanding of grapevines and vineyards and John 15, did it start to click. This is one of those "Light Bulb Moments" for me. What do you think "the desire of his heart" is for the Founder of the vineyard in our little winery story? Go and ask the "gorgeous young man" that Cherril will mention. The "desire of his heart" is obvious. All of his life since he was a young boy he had a passion for grapes. In the tour he mentioned this. All he ever wanted to be was a wine master for a vineyard.

Every character in our "perfect winery example"—or let's call it a "normal" winery—has the same passion. Every one of them is a branch of the same vine, and they have a passion to see the branches on their vines produce lots of quality grapes. Ask any of those working for the vineyard this question, "*You will ask what you desire, and it shall be done for you.*" What do you think they will all ask for? Do you think that perhaps their request has been answered?

In order to get back a "normal" Church perhaps we need to get back to basics. A functioning and productive winery may hold the key.

We see many varieties of grapes but all from the vine. We see many sizes of vineyards, but all with the purpose of producing grapes. Regardless of size or variety we do see structure. Embedded in this structure we see a passion about the product they produce.

EXIT 10

WHY CHURCH?

Why do I need Church? The better question is, "Why do I not want to be part of a *functional* Church family?"

Many times we do not have an answer to this question, "Why do I need Church?" so the immediate answer often is, "I am all churched out." Sounds like an answer, but really it is nothing but a pointless statement of despair. This comment *really* means that the person making the comment does not understand what Church is meant to be. If Church has a real purpose to a healthy Christian life, then they haven't found it.

It would also be as ridiculous to make the statement, "I am all familied out." Sometimes you may feel this as well, but in the end we all cherish and need family. Perhaps we need to simplify the question of Church and ask an even more basic question: "Why do I need a family?" The better question is, "Why do I not want to be part of a *functional* family?"

Notice the word *functional* in the above two statements. More and more today we hear and see *dysfunctional* families. A dysfunctional family shows all sorts of weak points and signs of stresses in the relationships. Can the Church, our family of God, be any different from our biological families?

God created humans to be social in nature. From the start it is very evident that God intended mankind to not be alone. The opening of Genesis states, *"So God created man in His own image; in the image of God He created him; male and female He created them. Then God blessed them"* (Genesis 1:27-28 NKJV).

Adam and Eve also had closeness with God as they walked in the garden each day. *"And they heard the sound of the Lord God walking in the garden in the cool of the day"* (Genesis 2:8 NKJV). It was important to God to have family relationships with Adam and Eve. The main reason God created them in his image was to have fellowship. I have often thought what an awesome experience to be able to be so close to God that you could feel and hear his presence in an atmosphere of perfect peace. What a terrible tragedy when humans messed this relationship up.

It is exciting to know that we are created in the image of God, and this is why God created male and female and didn't just come up with some other plan of a bunch of lone rangers wandering the earth. Again, it is very evident that God created man as a social creature and created us to not be alone. God intended us to be part of a functional family and part of a functional Church.

"And the LORD God said, 'It is not good that man should be alone; I will make him a helper comparable to him'" (Genesis 2:18 NKJV).

So why the comment and the feeling that "I am all churched out?" Right from the top on down, from the pastors and leaders to the newest believer attending the Church, we have missed the point that Church is a body and a family. I thought this would be a good place to go on a rabbit trail and attempt to define a functional family versus a dysfunctional family. It became very apparent that this is not a simple topic, and is the topic of many books on its own. The study of that topic will be left up to you, but I am sure you are getting my point.

The problem is this: Church has been permitted to slide into becoming an institution that needs members to support the activities of the institution. The institution has a number of employees who are to administer the much-needed programs of the Church in order to facilitate Church growth. The direction of the institution is mandated by the executives and employees with little personal communication to its members. Even though the appearance of the organization is to serve its members and achieve growth, the members feel alienated. The members are expected to be volunteers to support the programs administered by the staff. Miss the body concept, and we have missed the whole point of a healthy Church. Miss the key points in our families and we have a dysfunctional family.

Activity becomes empty with a lot of work, and eventually the supporters of the institution grow weary of it. The leaders of the institution come up with projects and programs that they feel the institution should include as part of their mission. Notice this point; the leaders in an effort to achieve Church growth come up with programs that will supposedly bring about growth. In most cases the "New Concept" for growth is not well thought-out or communicated to the average folk. The adherents of the organization are not included or made to feel a part of the programs but are simply told what they are expected to do. They are, however, expected to be a supporter of the institution. To work for an institution out of duty is far different than working for your family as a family member—or as scripture describes it, taking care of your body.

Once again, scripture defines this concept very well:

> 4 *"There are diversities of gifts, but the same Spirit.* 5 *There are*
> *differences of ministries, but the same Lord.* 6 *And there are*
> *diversities of activities, but it is the same God who works all*

> *in all. [7]But the manifestation of the Spirit is given to each one for the profit of all: [8] for to one is given the word of wisdom through the Spirit, to another the word of knowledge through the same Spirit, [9]to another faith by the same Spirit, to another gifts of healings by the same Spirit, [10]to another the working of miracles, to another prophecy, to another discerning of spirits, to another different kinds of tongues, to another the interpretation of tongues. [11]But one and the same Spirit works all these things, distributing to each one individually as He wills. [12]For as the body is one and has many members, but all the members of that one body, being many, are one body, so also is Christ. [13]For by one Spirit we were all baptized into one body—whether Jews or Greeks, whether slaves or free—and have all been made to drink into one Spirit. [14]For in fact the body is not one member but many"* (1 Corinthians 12:4-14 NKJV).

The concept of a body and the fact that *"the manifestation of the Spirit is given to each one for the profit of all"* is a far different model than the way many Churches function. Rather than allowing the individual giftings and attributes to be cultivated and grown, the organization develops a number of duties that must be performed by and accepted by the members.

Over the years, Cherril and I have been given the privilege of being part of people's lives (adults and youth) who for various reasons don't feel as if they have a family. In some cases these special friends, in fact, do not have a family. All sorts of problems and issues are evident with these that have come into our lives. Some feel a loss of direction, hopelessness, and even sickness caused by nothing more than the feeling that they do not belong to a family. It is very rewarding to look back and see the progress in their lives—purely because they feel that they have a purpose and belong to a family and that someone cares.

It is an established medical fact that loneliness can lead to depression and depression creates a feeling of loneliness. Research this fact for yourself and you may be surprised at your findings. Many websites are devoted to the one topic of depression. A simple search of "loneliness" may give you some insight into depression and the shocking fact that depression can and does also attack Christians. Loneliness is a very real condition and to our surprise is evident in many Churches.

Comments in medical journals read as follows: "Studies have shown loneliness can send a person down a path toward bad health, and even more intense loneliness. But while some have assumed the culprit was a dearth of others to remind a person to take care of himself or herself, new research suggests there's a direct biological link between being lonely and ill health. Lonely people have blood pressure readings as much as 30 points higher than non-lonely people, said the study leaders Louise Hawkley and Christopher Masi. Blood pressure differences between lonely and non-lonely people were smallest at age 50 and greatest among the oldest people tested. John Cacioppo, a University of Chicago social psychologist who studies the biological effects of loneliness, presented some of his latest research at the Society for Personality and Social Psychology meeting in San Diego in January. He has found, for instance, loneliness is tied to hardening of the arteries (which leads to high blood pressure), inflammation in the body, and even problems with learning and memory" (*Why Loneliness Can Be Deadly* by Katharine Gammon, LiveScience Contributor; March 2, 2012)

Can it be that God in his wisdom created people to need family and friends and Church? What better place for a person to find family and friends, than in the Church? But in many Church "bodies" this concept seems to have been totally missed. In an attempt to achieve numerical growth, many leaders are, in actual fact, impeding personal growth. Kind of a vicious cycle.

One of the most important functions of a good, healthy, and caring Church should therefore be to facilitate the opportunity to form good and positive friendships. Not the phony variety, but a real atmosphere of caring and supporting one another. No wonder scripture refers to the Church as the body of Christ.

Being part of a family is important and has great value. I think the great value of family can be demonstrated at Christmas. On the flip side of this statement however, is the fact that loneliness and depression are at a very high point at Christmas, with an unusually high incidence of suicide. Wow! Doesn't that thought throw a wet blanket on the festivities. The most depressing season for some is Christmas. Why? Some are so alone at a time that is meant to be a family celebration that they fall into a deep depression and a feeling that no one cares. Sound familiar?

Christmas is a big deal in our family. It is celebrated with about 40 to 50 of us gathered together for a big feast. It isn't always possible for the whole family to attend for various reasons, and they are missed. We don't have to push and promote the event. It is just expected that all who are able to will be coming to join in the celebrations. Crazy traditions develop over the years, and it is a family time that is looked forward to with lots of excitement and planning.

Talk about crazy traditions. For the last number of years the activity of eating has turned into a sporting event for the young guys in our family. About 10 or 12 of the guys drag out the bathroom scale and have a big weigh-in. The weights are recorded, to avoid cheating—not that any would cheat—and pictures are taken. The anticipated feast is placed on the table, consisting of a couple of large turkeys, and a ton of special dishes that the ladies have prepared. Now for the feast! Lots of laughing, joking, and good family time together.

When everyone has had their fill, then the same group of guys that participated in the weigh-in goes back to the scale and gets their full weights recorded. Sort of like weighing trucks with the Tare Weight and the Gross Weight. The guy who has the greatest increase in weight wins, and gets to go for desert first. "Good grief," you say, "Must be a bunch of barbarians!" Not at all, just a bunch of young, strong, and excited "barbarian" guys with huge appetites who have found a new way to have fun and compete. Everything in our family seems to turn into a competition.

Get my point? Not all families are the same, or have the same dynamics. I would consider our family to be a functional family—others may disagree—but we are not the same as all families. Good family relationships mean a place for every member of the family, from great-grandparents to the most recent baby, all are part of the excitement and family. We may be different than many families, and we have some weird wrinkles, but we are a functional family. No one is excluded, and no one wants to miss out. God made us this way, and I for one am glad, and I personally will do everything in my power to keep our family functioning this way!

How about Church? Does everything that happens in a Church need to be so regulated and made to conform to only "spiritual activities"? By the way, what are "spiritual activities"? Would it hurt to let our hair down once in a while and just act like a family rather than a religious institution?

So back to the question, "Why Church?" I guess the best answer is really the fact that it is a body that is not merely suggested by God, but created and ordained by God. Church is meant to be a well-planned body, directed by God to be an integral part of our walk as Christians. Church is not a new thing that was dreamed up as another organization that we should become a member of, but a living body that is designed by God to give us a sense of community and family. The real point of Church is that it is ordained and designed by God, and is important to him as the "family of God." We don't have to be theologians to figure out that God wants us to be part of a functional Church family.

Come back to our family Christmas scene for a second. We don't have a problem with family members not wanting to attend, and we don't have to block the Exits to prevent them from leaving prematurely. When you think of the young guys and the weigh-in, some most likely couldn't leave if they wanted to—most likely they couldn't even move as they are so stuffed! Our fun goes on into the night with crazy games and all sorts of stuff that only our family can relate to. That is the point. We are our family and we have our weird kinks, but this is us.

Many times, the Christmas celebrations have included those who are not born into our family, but have been included to become a part. These are the ones that have no family at Christmas. Crazy thing! They also enjoy our crazy fun times, and are more than glad to attend. Get my point? It is amazing the number of times we get comments such as, "Can we be a part of your family?" Sometimes in joking, but sometimes I think the statement is serious. Why?

What is deficient in some of our Churches today that is causing so many to exit? Perhaps we should consider the following quote from one more knowledgeable than I. Of particular note is that the problem does not seem to be a new problem. The quote was penned at some point in the 1950s.

"This is the tragedy and woe of the hour—which we neglect. The most important One who could possibly be in our midst—the Holy Spirit of God. Then, in order to make up for His absence, we have to do something to keep up our own spirits."… "I remind you that there are Churches so completely out of the hands of God that if the Holy Spirit withdrew from them, they wouldn't find it out for many months" (A.W. Tozer, from *Tozer Pulpit*, at www.goodreads.com A.W. Tozer > Quotes > Quotable Quote)

In the absence of a healthy spiritual condition, the leaders of the Church opt for programs and activities rather than settling down to the real purpose of the Church. This sounds like I am giving the leaders of the Church a "bum rap," but read the following passage carefully:

> *"But when the chief priests and scribes saw the wonderful things that He did, and the children crying out in the temple and saying, 'Hosanna to the Son of David!'* ***they were indignant****"* (Matthew 21:15 NKJV).

Can you imagine such a statement? Jesus shuts the programs and noise down and gets back to basics, heals a bunch of people. When was the last time you saw miracles in some of our churches? I would love to see this in our Churches. Some leaders may not be excited that revival has come with Almighty God walking into their temple. If revival does come into the Church then the "kings" feel excluded and want to own it. They are ticked off because their ego and place of authority are bruised. Their very aggressive fund-raising programs of selling their stuff to raise cash for some "much-needed projects" are shut down.

My email dialogue to a former youth pastor whom I have not seen since about 1968 may draw some focus on these comments. My question was asked of my friend in 2013 about a church condition around 1965 - 1967. In case you feel that only the pastors are a challenge, then read this dialogue. If you assume that the 1960's where the "Good Old Days" and all was well in the old days then read on. Some things just never seem to change.

My question: I was wondering if you would be interested in going a way back into the vaults of your mind? I am writing a book called EXITS about the reasons people choose to leave church. I would be interested in any thoughts you have of your time at the ----- church, Vancouver, B.C. I was fortunate to have been your friend and part of the youth group that you were pastoring. We had some great times and we had some challenges.

More on this in the Last chapter. This is a preview that fits well with the current point.

Once back home I reconnected with my home church. In the late 60's we saw a move of God in our church. We had a visiting youth evangelist visit and the youth group was mobilized to reach out to the unsaved. Now a new problem. A lot of *undesirable* types got saved and decided to attend our church. I was the youth leader at the time, and I found myself involved in this tempest. The leaders decided that some changes needed to be made. Eventually they were successful and the attendance of the youth was failing. [*I wonder why?*] Once again the leaders decided that the problem needed to be fixed. We had no paid staff for youth. That problem was resolved and the first paid youth pastor joined our staff. He was a great guy and became a good friend.

My friends reply in July of 2013 - Grant, I have been aware of your request but didn't want to flippantly answer. So after some time, prayer, and consideration, here goes. EXITS, the scripture says, 'How can two walk together except they be agreed'. Your passage shared with me, described the reason for our exit. 'Undesirable Types were getting saved'. That categorization in itself described the problem. Any soul embracing the saviour is precious, yet *'The Board'* fought us constantly to restrain our embracing of the outreach ministry. I shared a message one Sunday night, (I remember because of how scared I was to share it yet, Pastor B---- said I had to). The gist of it from Isaiah, was either we get on board with God's move or we would become a byword, a thing of history and nothing relevant. I'll let you judge the veracity of that, I won't. But after two years of the board fighting us Pastor B---- said, 'We need to move on, what we vision will never happen here. The board won't let it. I do thank God for elders like P------ W---- who truly saw and embraced the vision of a downtown outreach, praise and worship center. But they were not strong enough to combat the board whose desire was more societal minded than evangelical. Thus, the exit. Hope this helps. Always good hearing from you. Blessings, G---

As a follow up - The church just continued to dwindle away until by about the early 1990's the church just faded away and ceased to exist. To be continued in the closing chapter.

I have heard comments that "experts" on Church growth state that a good service should not last more than 60 minutes. If the Holy Spirit decides to visit, he is ushered out as we don't have time for the Holy Spirit. We have to stay within the appointed timing.

The nerve of Jesus to pull off such a stunt! In the absence of good spiritual health, the leaders of the Church opted to stroke their egos by creating lots of activity and raising lots of money, so that they could justify their presence and manifest their authority.

What then is the real purpose of the Church? Jesus by his own statement made it perfectly clear what the Church is meant to be: *"It is written,* ***'My house shall be called a house of prayer'****"* (Matthew 21:13 NKJV). This statement made by Jesus is a direct quote from Isaiah.

Has the purpose of the Church now changed?

> 6 *"Also the sons of the foreigner who join themselves to the Lord, to serve Him, and to love the name of the Lord, to be His servants—everyone who keeps from defiling the Sabbath, and holds fast My covenant—* 7 *even them I will bring to My holy mountain, and make them joyful in <u>My house of prayer</u>. Their burnt offerings and their sacrifices will be accepted on*

*My altar; **for My house shall be called a house of prayer for all nations**"* (Isaiah 56:6-7 NKJV).

The prophecy also brings to light some emotions that, in some cases, are lacking in some Churches. The people will be joyful and their offerings will be acceptable. Sounds fantastic!

If Church is not a body ordained by God, then why is there so much scripture written on the organization, leadership, and the purpose of the Church? The purpose of the Church was spoken of by Isaiah and the initial start-up of what is the Church body was detailed in Exodus 25—and every city Paul witnessed in, he established churches for the new believers, appointed elders, etc.

I have a copy of an "Audio Bible" and I like to listen to the scriptures sometimes, rather than reading it. I did this the other day and started listening to Exodus commencing with Exodus 25 onward. I listened to God speak to Moses giving the instructions of how to set up the first church building. Being a developer I found the instructions for building the "Tabernacle" to be very detailed and real cool! Listening to the voices was sort of like standing outside of the room and eavesdropping. (My wife often draws this to my attention: that I tend to eavesdrop—especially in restaurants.)

The instructions in this chapter start out by giving *everyone an opportunity* to participate in the building up of the new Church. No big hard-sell to give. No pressure for the building program but the simple comment by God: *"Speak to the children of Israel, that they bring Me an offering. From everyone who gives it willingly with his heart you shall take My offering*" (Exodus 25:2 NKJV).

It is obvious that God only wanted those who were willing participants, and not pressured participants, to take part in the building of the Tabernacle. Pressure tactics to increase giving are not part of a healthy Church.

Most of our family is in the construction business. (That may explain some of the big guys, and the huge appetites.) We know the mess that is created when people attempt to build a project without adequate plans. Even worse, attempting to build something with NO Plans. Not good! God is also well aware of this fact, and provided Moses and Aaron with some very detailed plans. In this translation the plans are referred to as the "pattern." The instructions start with the statement: *"Let them make Me a sanctuary, that I may dwell among them. According to all that I show you, that is, <u>the **pattern** of the tabernacle and the **pattern** of all its furnishings</u>, just so you shall make it"* (Exodus 25:8-9 NKJV).

The pattern is very detailed and well-explained. So much so, that you can take this detail to an architect and a builder and have current building plans produced to an exact scale. The modern New Testament Church has also been given a pattern, but for some reason we fail to use God's plans and have devised many other models. Can this also be part of the "all churched-out" feeling?

A couple of cool side points to demonstrate just how detailed these plans are. When I was a kid, a series of studies was being taught about the "Tabernacle and its Furniture" and the purpose of the Tabernacle. My uncle George decided that he would draw up a set of plans, and build a scale model of the Tabernacle and the furnishings to give a visual of Exodus 25. It was amazing and no detail was missed. It brought the teaching and the sermons to life, giving us the opportunity to actually see the Tabernacle.

Even more recently, the pastor of the Church that my son Lance and his family attend was speaking on the furniture of the Tabernacle. Lance, being in construction, was requested to build a full-scale model of the Tabernacle furnishings. A set of plans were drawn up from Exodus and our shop fired up to start the project. Get my point? God gives very specific plans concerning the structure of the Tabernacle—the Church of that day and also the Church of today.

God even gives details as to the form of worship in the Tabernacle. We no longer sacrifice animals in our services—it's very messy, and I am sure Green Peace or some organization would have a protest group at our doors if we did. Look at the detail of how to prepare the sacrifices and the duties of the priests. Even the little piece of fat that is attached to the liver of the animal is mentioned with instructions on how it is to be used in worship. Now that is detailed.

Sticking to the basics and the plan was the key to success for Israel if they were to prosper and be satisfied in their Church. All through the scriptures this is evident. Follow the plan and Israel prospers. Deviate from the plan and Israel is taken into bondage. What didn't they get or what don't we get?

Okay, I have made my point that God likes us to work with his plans. This is Old Testament and we are now New Testament. We are now free from the Law and we are under Grace. Yes, praise the Lord! What a great blessing when God gave to us a detailed plan for Church through the four gospels, the Acts of the Apostles, and Romans. These great scriptures are built on the foundation of the Old Testament, and the other books of the New Testament add details to the plans and their "supporting notes" to the participants.

Did you know that when an architect gives us a set of plans for a building that they attach the supporting notes and documents? The scriptures are no different. All we have to do is follow the plan and the notes to the plan will yield a well-built building. Many times when a person who does not understand building plans attempts to build a structure on their own, problems arise—BIG

TIME! Why? They only go according to the plans, but fail to read the specifications and details. Church is the same.

As we read through the New Testament scriptures we also see great details as to the structure, purpose, and organization of our modern Church. And once again, just as with Israel, we see the same results. Follow the plans as God instructed and flourish. Deviate from the plan and founder.

Founder is another nautical term (of a ship) and it means, "Fill with water and sink," For example, "Six drowned when the yacht foundered off the West coast." Not a good term, so why do we keep trying our own plans? Slow learners, I guess.

Does our modern Church come with a manual and operating instructions? Yes, it does. A different structure than the Old Testament Tabernacle but a definite plan all the same. It is also very clear that we as Christians are to participate in a Church as a "Body of Believers".

Structure is not the whole solution to the Exit challenge. We must bear the responsibility for our desire and will to follow a life that is pleasing to God. Our spiritual condition is not all external and subject to outside conditions. The condition of our hearts is between us and God, and we also have warnings in scripture about not getting a condition known as a cold heart.

As far as the Church goes, the instructions should work for any Church in any culture, of any size, in any geographic region. Churches come in all sizes shapes and flavors. But the reason God gives us instructions on Church is because it is important.

I am sure we have all heard or read instructions on Church growth but they don't work for all circumstances. The books tend to be very specific, depending on the writer's point of view. Big Church, no Church, no structure, huge structure, hang-loose, or uptight Church. Leave your current Church and start a new organization. Leave your current Church and start something with no plan or structure. Make sure the timing of the service does not exceed 60 minutes. The list of great ideas to achieve growth is endless.

God's plan for the Church is designed by him so that one plan fits all. The plan worked 2,000 years ago in the Middle East, worked a few years ago in the 1500s and will still work today in North America. It will work in faraway lands when our missionaries evangelize.

In this chapter I am not advocating you leave your Church and attempt to set up some new structure or organization. Don't throw out what you have and look for some new form of organization. Just read the manual—God's Word—and get what you already have working.

Something that drives me nuts is seeing a piece of equipment that is not operating to its specifications or potential. A good example is a DVD player with the clock flashing. How can the owner put up with this constant flashing showing "12:00 – 12:00 – 12:00" repeatedly? There is nothing wrong with the appliance, but there is something wrong big time with the owner! The fix is simple. Just pull out the manual, adjust a couple of buttons, and just like magic, no blinking *and* you can see the correct time.

If you are a pastor or Church leader then I encourage you to just pull out the manual. I am sure you will find that if you start to operate the equipment according to the manual you will find that things run a lot smoother. Communicate with those in your care as to why you are looking to make some adjustments to get back to basics.

It is amazing to me, but for some reason pastors and leaders can be such great communicators from the platform. But when it comes to important family matters like direction and the reason why things are done a certain way, then communication falls into a huge blackout. Why is that? I guess the family members are not capable of understanding such huge and weighty matters.

If you are not a pastor, then communicate with your pastor and give him or her the assurance that you are praying for them and wish to see the Church get back to the manual. Take some of the pressure off to achieve Church growth, get back to stopping the flashing DVD, and get back to Church health.

Who is the Church intended for?

Right from the get-go, do we have a clear vision of what the Church is? If not, then how can we reach the goal if the goal is not defined?

When God gave the instructions for the construction of the Tabernacle in Exodus, who was it meant to serve? It was to provide a place and a focal point for the nation of Israel to worship God. It provided the space and the furnishings for the priests of Israel to perform their appointed roles as instructed by God. It wasn't intended or designed as a facility that would be the outreach center for Israel to seek new members from the Philistine community (the Gentiles). A process was in place if a person chose to become a Jew, but the purpose of the Tabernacle was not to convert the Gentiles. Yes, a Gentile can convert to be a Jew and be accepted as a Jew.

I am going to get myself in trouble here because I will be misunderstood. It is not all that uncommon, however, for me to get myself into trouble. But allow me to say this: the primary purpose of Church is to provide a coming together of Christians to pray, worship, and study and be taught scripture.

> [23] *"Let us hold fast the confession of our hope without wavering, for He who promised is faithful.* [24]*And let us consider one another in order to stir up love and good works,* [25]*not forsaking the assembling of ourselves together, as is the manner of some, but exhorting one another, and so much the more as you see the Day approaching"* (Hebrews 10:23-25 NKJV).

It appears pretty clear that Hebrews 10 is directed to Christians. Yes, non-believers are more than welcome to attend Church. Non-believers will come to Church and hear the gospel. For sure we pray they will! And for sure the Church will provide access points for the non-believers to hear the salvation gospel. The prime purpose, however, of the main Sunday meeting is the assembling together as described in Hebrews 10. It is to be dedicated to Christians and not the unbeliever.

Often I hear the phrase "I am not getting fed at my Church." Sometimes this may be true, but what is the comment really saying? We tend to hear the same basic preaching over and over because the preaching and teaching is directed to the lost and not to the believer. Would it not be better to encourage spiritual growth so that the believers of the Church are healthy and better equipped to encourage growth and the believers winning souls? It seems evident that in Acts 2 and other scriptures that the Church growth was caused by evangelism as a personal approach. One on one, friend to friend, worker to worker, and then the new believers coming together with the established believers to be taught and mentored. Yes, there were public meetings and evangelistic sermons by the apostles. But I am certain the "word of mouth" approach was also a big factor.

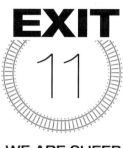

EXIT 11

WE ARE SHEEP

NOW THIS IS A HUMBLING STATEMENT. WE ARE NOTHING BUT A bunch of sheep. This can be a real pride-crusher, or it can be a big learning experience. Many will not grasp the whole meaning of this comparison, because not many have had the opportunity to work with or learn about sheep.

Many of the teachings of Jesus—and of scripture in general—can be lost because of our modern life styles. When was the last time you were on a farm, or when was the last time you spent any time studying livestock? At the time Jesus walked on Earth, agriculture was an integral part of most people's lifestyle. In our current city culture, livestock is simply some smelly activity that takes place someplace in the country. We buy our produce, dairy and meat products in plastic trays covered in plastic wrap with a nice tidy label from our favorite supermarket. Lately the rage is to buy organic. Even *that* term is a bit mysterious. The knowledge of how agricultural products are produced is a foreign topic. Yet much can be learned from understanding the basic concepts of agriculture in scripture.

Next time you are in a line-up at Costco, watch the people. The checkout line is seemingly not moving. One line appears to be stagnant and getting longer by the minute. A new checkout is opened and one brave person makes a move and then the whole bunch bolts to follow. Takes only one sheep to do something and the whole flock follows. You can recognize the expressions and almost hear the bleating. Perhaps a basic understanding of sheep will give us some insight into how to keep some of our Church's lambs from exiting.

I love the way scripture uses stories to help us understand a topic that is not familiar to us. Jesus in particular did this when telling parables. A parable conveys a meaning indirectly by the use of comparison, analogy, or the like. Some of the parables of Jesus are based on actual accounts, and some are analogies that are designed to help us understand a basic principle of our Christian life and Church in general.

I have the opportunity to teach or public speak on various topics from time to time. Many times, while working with a business client I realize that the point they need to understand in order to move forward is outside of their knowledge base. I have learned to recognize these blank faces and the glazed-over eyes and their body language that says, "What on earth are you talking about?" I give them a little story and then we get a breakthrough with one of those Aha moments! To coin a phrase, "The light goes on." Once the light is switched on we can move forward.

Sitting down and writing many of the comments in this book is turning out to be an AHA! moment for me as well. It seems like we sheep have a difficult time discerning a simple challenge in our Churches. We see the same problems cycling over and over and yet the answers are in the scripture.

The concept of sheep-herding in our Churches is taken from my notes when I talked about this topic almost 18 years ago at a speaking opportunity. Some of this topic is from a sermon that I heard almost 40 years ago. I think the lessons were relevant then and must be relevant now because the same problems keep rearing up. Nothing has changed. Let's try for an AHA! moment, and see the light turn on.

WE ARE COMPARED TO SHEEP: In the New Testament, Jesus used many parables and stories to emphasize points in his messages. Throughout scripture Christians are compared to sheep. In the Old Testament, once again we are compared to sheep. All you have to do is learn a little about sheep and you will see why this is such a fitting comparison. One of the most well known scriptures of the relationship of a sheep with its shepherd is:

---

1 *"The Lord is my shepherd; I shall not want.* 2 *He makes me to lie down in green pastures; He leads me beside the still waters.*
3 *He restores my soul; He leads me in the paths of righteousness For His name's sake.* 4 *Yea, though I walk through the valley of the shadow of death, I will fear no evil; For You are with me; Your rod and Your staff, they comfort me.* 5 *You prepare a table before me in the presence of my enemies; You anoint my head with oil; My cup runs over.* 6 *Surely goodness and mercy shall follow me All the days of my life; And I will dwell in the house of the Lord forever"* (Psalms 23:1-6 NKJV).

To get off on the right foot (all four of them) let's ruminate on Psalm 23 for a few minutes. Ruminants are characterized by their four chambered stomach and "cud-chewing" behavior. I don't know Hebrew or Greek, so I thought to throw some livestock terms in to impress the readers.

Next time you are stressed out from your fast life in the city, take a trip to the country. Locate a flock of sheep in a grassy meadow and just watch them as they lay in the shade and ruminate. A very peaceful scene. While you are taking your sheep break read the 23rd Psalm and see if you find new meaning in it.

This is a good time to change lenses on our points of view. Many times our viewpoint is restricted by our current life style, our circumstances, or our background. Our tendency is to look at things from the vantage point of what we are currently experiencing and where we are standing. Further to this, most sheep tend to look at the two hours on Sunday morning as the total Church experience. Church, however, is more than just Sunday morning service. It is very deeply wrapped in the whole "flock" experience—or lack of it. If you are an old sheep and have been in Church life for a lot of years you will have some Church experience that marks the high point of your Christian walk.

Perhaps as a kid you used a magnifying glass to focus the sun's rays onto a piece of wood until it started to smoke and burn. A magnifying glass is nothing more than a lens. Much like the magnifying glass, the lens of my mind will take the positive rays of my past experiences and focus these memories on a very fine point in time. The focal point of these memories will in some fashion become my normal. When a person has come from an unfortunate background their lens may focus on the negative. If they focus on these negative experiences long enough depression and ill health is the result. Be careful how you use your magnifying glass to focus the sun. Are you focusing on the positive or negative?

As I stated earlier, if one Church plan is to fit all, then we must look beyond our current Church experience. If you are attending a "large" rural Church, it may be different than a "large" city Church. If you are in a smaller community then your Church lens will focus on your current size of Church. If you are a new Christian and have no Church background, then what will your lens focus on? The point is that if Church is to work, then no matter the geographical position of your Church, the culture of your Church, or the time in history of your Church, the same manual will provide a standard to follow.

Our home group watched a video study focusing on the Seven Churches of Revelation. This is a refreshing walk through Revelation focusing on the characteristics and culture of each of the seven Churches. I strongly recommend this series to get a fresh perspective on the book of Revelation and Jesus' message to Churches in all times. Travel to the land of the Bible with host Joe Stowell to visit the ancient sites of the seven churches described in Revelation. Gain insights into God's love for the world, His warning and correction for the churches, and His hope and encouragement for the future. A perfect resource for individual or small group study. It's produced by Day of Discovery.

These were very real and active Churches almost 2,000 years ago. Recorded and written in AD 95, as a matter of fact. They are very old and no longer alive but the history of these Churches is a mirror image of our Churches today. Amazing thought: we are not any different today from a global perspective.

In the Fall my son, Lance and I travel to northern B.C. for hunting season. In most of the small towns and villages up north an absence of church buildings is very apparent. I am sure there are believers in these communities, so what does Church look like for them? No doubt the same challenges but only a different scale. We have since come to learn that even though they have no church building in a certain town, they do have Church. I discovered that one group meets at a rancher's house. Just like the New Testament Church. A few books have been written establishing the fact that if we want to be a New Testament Church then we need to get rid of our current Church model and meet in private houses. Looking through this lens then the conclusion will be that we should all move up north to this town and become part of the "Ranch Church."

Just a random thought: do you ever wonder why Church plants tend to mainly focus on large urban areas and communities? When was the last time you heard of a new Church plant seeking out one of these smaller northern communities with little or no Christian influence? In our neighborhood almost every school, and many street corners, have church buildings with a group of believers meeting on Sunday morning. Many are Church plants of existing Churches just down the road. When I travel up north, I see very few functioning Churches. Just wondering. Topic for another book or at least a chapter, perhaps.

The term "shepherd" is also interpreted to mean pastor. A pastor has a very important role in a functioning Church and is more than the "speaker on Sunday morning." Jesus recognized the importance of a pastor/shepherd. Read one of his comments as recorded in Matthew.

> 35 *"Then Jesus went about all the cities and villages, teaching in their synagogues, preaching the gospel of the kingdom, and healing every sickness and every disease among the people.* 36 *But when He saw the multitudes, He was moved with compassion for them, because they were weary and scattered, like sheep having no shepherd.* 37 *Then He said to His disciples, "The harvest truly is plentiful, but the laborers are few.* 38 *Therefore pray the Lord of the harvest to send out laborers into His harvest"* (Matthew 9:35-38 NKJV).

Many people were accepting Jesus as he was teaching and preaching throughout the country. Jesus recognized the need, however, for shepherds. With the number of people coming to accept Jesus he knew that groups of believers would be coming together to form Churches. Sheep have a natural instinct to flock together for protection.

A key point of this portion of scripture is usually missed in most sermons that I have heard. The lens of the preacher is focused on the unsaved harvest waiting to be harvested and brought into the barns. The preacher in most cases does not have his focus on the new lambs that are being born each day. You don't need a shepherd for unharvested grain, but you for sure need a shepherd for newborn lambs. Focus on his comment, *"He was moved with compassion for them, because they were weary and scattered, like sheep having no shepherd."*

What is the point of gathering up a bunch of harvesters and sending them out into the fields to bring in the harvest? It is great to have a great harvest, but not so great to see it fade away because no thought has been given to protecting and rearing the "harvest." Kind of dumb, when you think about it.

Churches are meant to be a body of believers. While on earth, however, Jesus could not be personally attending to the day-to-day needs of these new believers. Shepherds were needed for the budding Churches that would follow the birth of the new lambs. Jesus was aware of two problems when he made his comment. The sheer size and numbers of lambs were more than one man could handle. Secondly, and more importantly, Jesus would soon be leaving this Earth. Once Jesus would return to heaven, then who would look after the new lambs that were being born daily? Sheep do best when they have personal contact with their shepherd. It was intended that the Church would continue after his departure to heaven. There are many roles in a functioning, normal Church. An important role is the role of a pastor.

> [11] *"And He Himself gave some to be apostles, some prophets, some evangelists,* ***and some pastors*** *and teachers,* [12]*for the equipping of the saints for the work of ministry, for the edifying of the body of Christ,* [13]*till we all come to the unity of the faith*

and of the knowledge of the Son of God, to a perfect man, to the measure of the stature of the fullness of Christ; [14]that we should no longer be children, tossed to and fro and carried about with every wind of doctrine, by the trickery of men, in the cunning craftiness of deceitful plotting, [15]but, speaking the truth in love, may grow up in all things into Him who is the head—Christ— [16]from whom the whole body, joined and knit together by what every joint supplies, according to the effective working by which every part does its share, causes growth of the body for the edifying of itself in love" (Ephesians 4:11-16 NKJV).

We have pastors in most Churches, but the role of a pastor has become a bit fuzzy. Pastor has become a title that means that a person is on the payroll of the Church as an employee. Getting hired and paid by the Church organization immediately confers the title of pastor. The person speaking from the platform is often called the pastor of the Church. This may be true but there is more than this. A pastor is only one Church office, but in Ephesians we see that there are more ministry gifts. Why such a focus on the term "pastor," and so little focus on the other gifts? In many cases, the speaker of the assembly may, in fact, not be gifted as a pastor but is in fact an evangelist or a teacher.

A number of roles in the Church are defined in Ephesians. All of these roles are important to a healthy Church, and the pastor is only one of them. In order for this biblical concept to function well the pastor must have the support of the other parts of the body identified in Ephesians.

TO BE A SHEPHERD YOU MUST LIKE SHEEP. Now, that is a dumb statement, but you'd be surprised at how many don't. This also means that the shepherd wants to be with and mix with the sheep. How can a shepherd minister to the needs of the flock if the shepherd is not in intimate contact with the sheep?

> *"He will feed His flock like a shepherd; He will gather the lambs with His arm, and carry them in His bosom, and gently lead those who are with young"* (Isaiah 40:11 NKJV).

I am sure most have seen pictures of Jesus carrying a lamb. Have you ever thought about why we sometimes see a picture of a shepherd carrying a lamb on his shoulders or in his arms? A wayward sheep is a sheep that wanders from the flock into danger. Often this is a repeated behavior with a particular sheep, not a onetime occurrence. One of the roles of the shepherd is to set boundaries for his sheep. He knows what is healthy and good for them, and his boundaries are there for the protection and care of the sheep. If a lamb is wandering away from the flock and away from the care of the shepherd it is headed to a place that could be dangerous and hurtful. We now see a vivid picture that a shepherd is with his sheep more than just on the stage Sunday morning speaking to them.

The rod and the staff are used to keep them close and safe but sometimes that is not enough. The shepherd gives direction and correction to the sheep in his care. At times, however, sheep still choose to wander away from the safety and security to a place that is outside the boundaries set up for their protection.

When a lamb continues to wander away from the flock and shepherd and put itself at risk, a loving shepherd will take measures to keep the lamb safe. The shepherd may choose to carry the lamb and restrict its freedom. This forces the sheep to be dependent on the shepherd for care. It must remain in very close proximity to the shepherd where it will not only receive care, but where it will learn to recognize the shepherd's voice, see his love, and develop a relationship that was not being built when the sheep was wandering. The hope is that the sheep will learn that the shepherd's care brings safety, security, love, goodness, and peace.

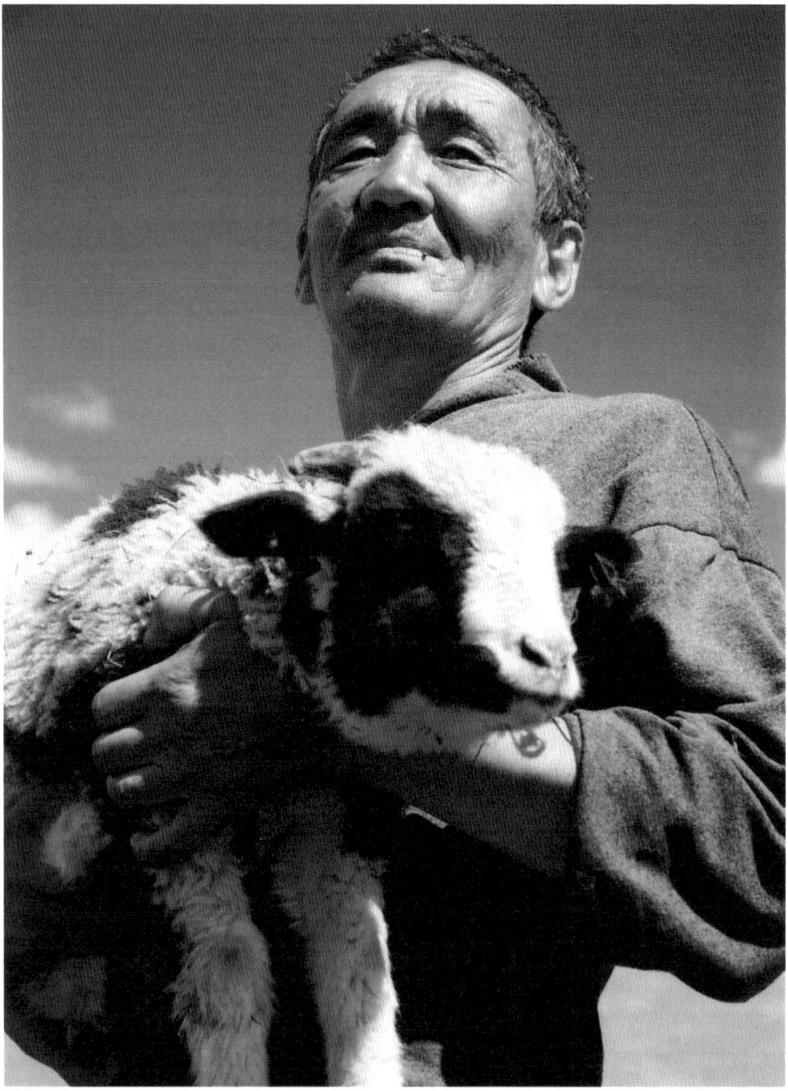

When a sheep goes missing, that sheep is indeed missed and some follow-up takes place. The shepherd will leave the main flock in the care of a shepherd-in-training and will go out and look for the lost sheep. He knows that one is missing because he knows the sheep personally. Plus, a quick count shows him that one sheep is missing from the flock.

[11] "For the Son of Man has come to save that which was lost. [12]"What do you think? If a man has a hundred sheep, and one of them goes astray, does he not leave the ninety-nine and go to the mountains to seek the one that is straying? [13]And if he should find it, assuredly, I say to you, he rejoices more over that sheep than over the ninety-nine that did not go astray. [14]Even so it is not the will of your Father who is in heaven that one of these little ones should perish" (Matthew 18:11-14 NKJV).

Now this image may pose a real problem when we think of the model that we see in many of our Churches.

What a shepherd is not! Now for a story about a guy who thought he was a shepherd but wasn't. As you will soon see, he had no regard for his sheep, but was only in it for the money. For a number of years, the pasture next to ours was rented to a sheep guy as summer pasture. This sheep guy also rented a number of similar pastures from land owners in our area. He owned a large number of sheep spread throughout the Valley. Rumor had it that he owned the greatest number of sheep in our area.

Each spring about mid-April about 50 ewes with lambs would be trucked to the pasture to spend the summer. They were given little care. They were not mistreated, but received no personal contact from the sheep guy. I am purposely not calling him a "shepherd," but the "sheep guy," and you will soon see why.

Often I would see a pile of wool lying in the field. I would go and inspect this white pile and it would be a dead sheep. The animal had obviously been the target of some predator, and was the meal left over from the previous night's kill. We don't have wolves in our area, but we do have lots of coyotes. Coyotes are predators and very clever and vicious hunters. You may have seen Wiley Coyote on the Bugs Bunny cartoons with your kids, but, as you might have guessed, this is not a good portrayal of a real life coyote. Do they still have Bugs Bunny cartoons? Some TV channels still carry those old reruns.

A few times I witnessed the hunt in progress. Not a pretty sight for city folk—or for any as far as that goes. Hunting and killing sheep is deadly business for these coyotes. With no shepherd in the field tending his sheep, the sheep and lambs didn't stand a chance. A couple of times I would see what was shaping up and come to the rescue of the sheep. The coyote in question soon became my prey. The coyote lost because I had an occasion to protect a sheep. Now with a dead coyote in the field, his brothers tended to bypass this pasture for a few weeks. Most often, however, this was not the case, as the coyote tends to hunt at night when the sheep are sleeping.

One day I saw the sheep guy coming to check on his sheep and drop off a few replacement sheep in the pasture. The new sheep in the field were to "top up" for the missing sheep that had become coyote lunch. I thought I would take this opportunity to go and have a chat and see what the problem was.

I told him what I had been witnessing and also wanted to know why he didn't come and remove the dead sheep when he became aware of their deaths. His comments were a bit startling, to say the least. He said that he used to have a smaller flock of sheep and had spent more time using more traditional methods. He had a sheep dog, and would have a llama with the sheep to help protect them. He had his own pasture and the required sheep pen and equipment. The problem was the falling price of wool. He couldn't make enough money with the more traditional methods. To look after a llama to attend the sheep at night would just add work and expense to his operations. In order to make a profit from his sheep, he needed to expand and reduce his costs.

He may have lost a few sheep each year to predators, but in his estimation, this was just the cost of doing business. A few dead sheep was much less costly than personal care of a smaller flock. If he left the dead ones in the field, the coyotes would kill fewer sheep as they would feed on a dead sheep for a few days, before they needed to kill again. Leaving the dead ones, in fact, prevented the man from losing even more sheep. Sound reasonable? With multiple pastures and multiple flocks of sheep, he could now turn a profit. His parting comment was, "They are only sheep and sheep are cheap."

As he jumped in his truck and drove away I thought, "This is only the sheep guy, and not a shepherd." It struck my heart as how similar this was to many of our Churches. "Sheep are cheap!" It is real tragedy when young lambs in a Church are left to fend for themselves and some don't make it.

I remember vividly a sermon taught by a pastor that I respected greatly, Lorne Pritchard. Unfortunately, he has since passed away but I still remember his words. He was teaching on the role of the pastor (shepherd) and described the sheep as the congregation in the Church. He said that it was not the role of the shepherd to produce lambs. It was the role of the shepherd to look after his sheep, protect his sheep, and feed his sheep. With a flock of healthy sheep, the shepherd could expect an increase of healthy new lambs every spring. The shepherd was not to focus on Church growth but on Church health. Keep healthy sheep and they will produce healthy lambs.

I can see this principle very clearly each spring. As I am writing this chapter, it is lambing season on our street. The shepherds take care of their sheep all year long and the new lambs appear each April.

Sheep are not like cattle. I have raised cattle and horses and I understand them well. Sheep, on the other hand, need to be led, fed, cared for, and protected from predators. They are not real smart and they have absolutely no defense system other than to run. Sheep are a prey animal. When they are faced with danger, their natural instinct is to flee, not fight. Their strategy is to use avoidance and rapid flight to avoid being eaten. (Their problem is that they are not too good at the "rapid flight" part either.) What a feeling to realize that you are born on this earth to be lunch.

We also have a number of coyotes in our area, and these love to feed on sheep. The shepherd is on a constant look out for predators. I try to do my part in controlling the coyote population as well. A few coyote casualties have taken place on our farm. All in the name of the sheep with a high incidence of lead poisoning on our property.

Each spring, just like clockwork, the pastures come to life with new lambs popping up. I have never seen the shepherd giving birth to a lamb, but I have seen the ewes giving birth to the lambs with the assistance of the shepherd. Get my point?

After an all-night fishing trip and a fish fry on the beach, Jesus gave this instruction in John 21:12-17 (NKJV):

> 15 *"So when they had eaten breakfast, Jesus said to Simon Peter, 'Simon, son of Jonah, do you love Me more than these?' He said to Him, 'Yes, Lord; You know that I love You.' He said to him,*
> ***'Feed My lambs.'*** 16 *He said to him again a second time, 'Simon, son of Jonah, do you love Me?' He said to Him, 'Yes, Lord; You know that I love You.' He said to him,*
> ***'Tend My sheep.'*** 17 *He said to him the third time, 'Simon, son of Jonah, do you love Me?' Peter was grieved because He said to him the third time, 'Do you love Me?' And he said to*

> *Him, 'Lord, You know all things; You know that I love You.'*
> *Jesus said to him,*
> ***'Feed My sheep.'"***

Jesus was talking to a bunch of fishermen who didn't understand sheep. Jesus also intended that these fishermen would be the future shepherds (pastors) of the New Testament Church. Notice the progression:

1. **"Feed my lambs."** The new Christians (the lambs). Feed them so that they will grow to be productive sheep. Focus on the care of the lambs as they will be your sheep for the future growth of the Church.
2. **"Tend my sheep."** A shepherd takes care of, and protects his sheep. (Watch over the established Christians to keep them safe.) They are the adults from last year's lambs, the established believers.
3. **"Feed my sheep."** Not only is the shepherd instructed to tend his sheep and keep them safe and give them good instruction, but he is also meant to feed the sheep. A good healthy diet will keep sheep healthy. Not exactly rocket science.

When the shepherd looks after this simple "circle of life" for sheep then there will be a healthy flock of sheep and once again each spring the sheep will bear a new flock of lambs. A healthy flock brings growth.

A term that is becoming quite common is "seeker-friendly service." Basically, the seeker-sensitive Church tries to reach out to the unsaved person by making the Church experience as comfortable, inviting, and non-threatening to him or her as possible. This may be comfortable for the non-believer, but what is happening to the already-saved sheep? Perhaps we need to re-examine the purpose of the main Sunday morning service. Is this service for the unsaved or for the sheep? In many models, the plan is to have the Church produce the lambs, as Church growth is key. The main reason they lack lambs, however, is that they have barren sheep.

With many modern models, Church is becoming more like a factory to produce lambs. Create activities and programs to attract the non-believer, give them a little bit of the gospel and just enough to hopefully keep them returning. Once they are in the door then we trust that we will produce a new flock of lambs. Part of the problem, however, is the abundance of underfed sheep and orphaned lambs. It is very unfortunate that many times a person appears to accept the Lord yet in a short period of time they are missing in action. The Sower and his Seed parable partially explain this phenomena but another factor may be in play here, and that is: we have sheep guys (not shepherds) producing orphaned lambs.

A non-believer comes to Church without having any personal contact with other believers. They hear the gospel and then choose to accept Jesus. Just as with lambs, the shepherd now must take some responsibility for these lambs to survive. The new lamb is taught and encouraged to separate themselves from their worldly connections, etc. So far, so good. No argument here. This they do, but they do not and did not have any personal connections with the Church when they made their decision. Because they have no "Christian parent" figure they become lonely, and are drawn back to their former support circle. In effect, they have been born into the Church to become an orphan and we see them head for the Exit. We are seeing lambs born without the support of an ewe or a shepherd.

What are we doing to help our orphan lambs be introduced to our flocks? It is always a thrilling experience to see someone attend Church and accept Jesus. But it is equally sad to see a new believer turn away and leave after a short time.

If this picture were not true then our Churches (sheep pens) should be bursting at the seams. I don't know how many revivals I have witnessed and seen literally hundreds of people come to Jesus at the front of the Church. Wow! Church growth is happening! But I have to ask, where are these new lambs now? I have done my part to shoot a few coyotes and protect a few lambs, but it is heartbreaking to see the cycle of lambs leaving. They are like a vapor. They appear at Church, sort of hang around the flock, and then like smoke they are gone. Where to?

Perhaps we need to get back to the model of a normal Church. Remember our discussion on what a normal Church looks like? Perhaps this may be a good time to go back and read again the portion on "what is normal." Once you have done that pull out the manual for a closer look.

For an ewe to do her job and be a good mother, her shepherd needs to intervene with support. What does scripture say about shepherds?

> *"But he who enters by the door is the shepherd of the sheep. To him the door keeper opens, and the sheep hear his voice; and he calls his own sheep by name and leads them out. And when he brings out his own sheep, he goes before them; and the sheep follow him, for they know his voice. Yet they will by no means follow a stranger, but will flee from him, for they do not know the voice of strangers"* (John 10:2-5 NKJV).

> *"Shepherd the flock of God which is among you, serving as overseers, not by compulsion but willingly, not for dishonest gain but eagerly; nor as being lords over those entrusted to you, but being examples to the flock"* (1 Peter 5:2-3 NKJV).

The above scriptures portray a very peaceful lifestyle of a shepherd caring for and allowing the sheep and lambs time to grow and feed. How do you feed sheep? They are a grazing animal as well as a ruminant. You must allow them time to graze and to lie down and chew their cud in peace. Without this they cannot digest their food and will actually be poorly nourished and get sick. You cannot keep them on the move. Sheep cannot be driven like cattle or ridden like horses. Sheep need to be at peace and they need consistency in their daily lives.

To review the characteristics of sheep, they are:

- Easily frightened and easy prey for predators
- Dependent on shepherds
- Get sick easily from stress
- Need consistency in their daily lives
- Need companionship and will follow the flock without thinking

Ewes can provide the babies with all the love and nourishment they need, but it is up to the shepherd to make sure the babies get a healthy start. The shepherd puts the ewe and her lamb into a small pen and cares for them, so the mother and baby can bond and get to know one another. They stay together for a few days, and then rejoin the rest of the flock. Without this bonding time the ewe and lamb may not bond to each other and the lamb suffers.

These comments may produce confusion and lead to a misunderstanding. At all times a Church must be conscious of the fact that non-believers will come to Church and be drawn by the Holy Spirit to seek out something that they feel they are missing. Others may be new believers who have accepted Jesus through some outside testimony, but now feel compelled to join a functioning flock.

Just as in the sheep world, any healthy flock will for sure have orphaned lambs. What to do?

Lamb Rearing 101: Once lambing season is upon us, we occasionally are left with orphan lambs, and they may need hand-rearing. Hand-rearing takes a lot of time and hard work, but can be very rewarding. At around six weeks of age the lambs can be gradually weaned off the milk substitute and onto the Lamb Starter Grower which can be fed to appetite as the milk is diminished and withdrawn from the diet.

> 1 *"Therefore, laying aside all malice, all deceit, hypocrisy, envy, and all evil speaking,* 2 *as newborn babes, desire the pure milk of the word, that you may grow thereby,* 3 *if indeed you have tasted that the Lord is gracious"* (1 Peter 2:1-3 NKJV).

It is up to the shepherd and the rest of the flock to help the new lamb get established. The only option for raising orphan lambs may be to bottle-feed your lamb. However, during these two days while you are trying to get your lamb to be accepted you must feed your lamb some colostrum as soon after birth as possible. If you don't do this your lamb will most likely die within a few days with a large clot in its gut. The colostrum is also very necessary as it contains antibodies that will protect the lamb from disease and acts as a laxative to get rid of fecal matter. (Told you this sheep stuff is a messy business.) Colostrum is easy to get if you have other lambing ewes, as you can milk an ewe for the colostrum and place this in a bottle for your orphan lamb.

Throughout this whole process, lambs should be housed in a clean, warm environment with access to fresh clean water at all times. Plus, care should be taken with the depth of water to make sure they do not drown. Hand-reared lambs can either be turned out to graze or kept in with hay and concentrate. Just as with the new lambs, the new Christian must be incorporated seamlessly into their new family. It is up to the shepherd to make sure that this is the case and to assist as needed.

A key thing to remember about hand-rearing is that routine is very important and once started should be stuck to. Another key point for the survival of your lambs is hygiene—good hygiene standards in pens, and when storing milk substitute, and using feeders, is essential. *Consistency* is the key. You may have noticed this phrase throughout this book: "Consistency is the key" If consistency is so important in so many areas of basic life, then why do we struggle with this in our churches?

Note the reference in 1 Peter to the phrase *"pure milk of the word."* Stay clear of weird and confusing doctrinal issues, and new revelations and strange interpretations of scripture. Be careful what you feed your sheep. No genetically modified food here.

Looking after a weak or orphaned animal at birth is a lot of work but comes with huge rewards. I have had experience with this. When an animal was having trouble at birth, we have assisted it into this world. I can recall sleeping next to a newborn animal in our barn, with it wrapped in my clothing, to give it warmth from my body to keep it alive through the night. Okay, this is getting kind of sappy – I am a Red Neck guy!

So the question is, is it "Ministry" or "Program"? Do we as a Church, a flock of sheep, produce and promote programs that don't allow time for our sheep to grow and create relationships? Why is it that many people may come into a Church, accept the Lord, and then we don't see any sign of them a short time later? (Retaining our lambs is growth, remember.)

Why is it that Christians, after many years in a Church, come to the realization that they have few close friends and are running a bit ragged at the edges in their personal and family relationships? They keep incredibly busy in the Church, including being part of Church staff, but find that there are few if any real close and meaningful relationships. Then we wonder why we have casualties and burnout along the way. It has been said that business can be the death of a Church.

Are we shepherding our sheep or are we driving our sheep? There is a vast difference between the picture of a shepherd in a peaceful valley tending his sheep—as in the 23rd Psalm—and a cattle drive. A cattle drive creates all kinds of dust and noise and looks like a big deal. It doesn't, however, do anything for the cattle except get them to market. Even the cowboys get tired and worn out. Sheep react to stress differently. They die. If sheep are under a lot of stress the mortality rate increases big time. Stress your sheep and they may die. Simple fact of sheep life.

Are we involved in Church growth or sheep growth? In our zeal to build bigger and better sheep pens are we forgetting the real purpose—to produce lambs and sheep that are healthy and producing Christians?

What about Church growth? Let's go back to the shepherd and sheep story. How does a shepherd grow his flock? He keeps his sheep healthy and fed, so that they can produce lambs and then does everything possible to keep the lambs alive and healthy. Every Christian is to be a shepherd: Read John 21:14-17 carefully again. If you love the Lord you are to feed his lambs and sheep.

The weekly Sunday morning service should be primarily for the believer. This may be the one time for most of the flock to get together for some good grazing on a lush meadow. But perhaps an inventory should be taken to see if what we are feeding is producing good healthy sheep. It is what is taking place in the lives of the sheep, outside of the Church, that is the indication if our flocks are healthy.

- ✓ Am I a stronger and a more mature Christian than a year ago?
- ✓ Is my family stronger in the Lord than a year ago?
- ✓ Are my relationships with friends and relatives closer than a year ago?
- ✓ Have I encouraged my friends through relationships to walk a healthy walk with the Lord?
- ✓ Who have I shepherded or "mentored" this year?
- ✓ Who have I led to the Lord this year?
- ✓ Am I in close contact with this individual and do I support him or her?
- ✓ Am I closer to those that shepherd me and have I been a positive influence on them in return?
- ✓ If I haven't fed any lambs, kept any lambs from getting sick, or become a healthier sheep, then what is the point of what I have done?
- ✓ Do I contribute to a small group that becomes a caring community?
- ✓ Be ministry-focused, not program-driven.
- ✓ Allow people the freedom to say "No" to serving.
- ✓ Help people discover their spiritual gifts so they are energized by serving instead of becoming burned out.
- ✓ Train people so they can serve and implement their gifts.
- ✓ Take seriously your role in mentoring leaders.
- ✓ Be sensitive to family needs by not overbooking the church calendar or expecting that everyone will attend every event.
- ✓ Model authentic Christianity by allowing people to be real instead of having to pretend to have it all together.

- ✓ Pray for your family, friends, and pastors, that they will be genuine burden-bearers who honor Christ and bring help in times of stress.
- ✓

Now read Psalm 23 again and see if it has new meaning.

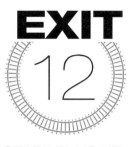

EXIT 12

STABILITY IS KEY

> [1] *"In the beginning God created the heavens and the earth.* [2] *The earth was without form, and void; and darkness was on the face of the deep. And the Spirit of God was hovering over the face of the waters"* (Genesis 1:1-2 NKJV).

IF GOD INTENDED OUR LIVES TO BE *"WITHOUT FORM, AND VOID,"* then he would have stopped Creation at the second verse in the first book. It must be that God looked at this point in Creation and said to himself, "If I leave my Creation at this point, it will drive me nuts!" God obviously had a more precise plan in mind for his Creation, his universe and man. As we look around God's universe we see that everything works better with structure, consistency, and focus. Watch any activity ranging from family, Church, to businesses. Without a consistent focus and structure it is usually experiencing challenges.

Consider for a moment a family that has little or no structure. You may be able to think of such a family. Hopefully, the family you think of is not yours. The day-to-day plan for our sample family is basically no plan. They are free spirits and living for the moment to see what the day brings. The day usually brings a series of unplanned events that come to cause pressures. Mom is running on a constant treadmill and at the end of the day she is approaching burnout mode, and crashes into bed at night totally exhausted.

Dad is under constant pressure to work a little harder and try to earn some extra cash. The day is long, and the breaks seem to be few. It seems like the list of uncompleted household chores is endless and never seems to be reduced. The day is long and about an hour after mom falls into bed, dad crashes after watching the late news (to keep up on the recent world tragedies). Sometimes he simply falls asleep on the couch. His night's sleep is short and restless.

Mom and dad wake early in the morning feeling like they just got to bed with little rest, and hit the floor running. They need to get an early start in order to be ready for the next set of random and unplanned events that are sure to need their full attention. Family time is some sort of mythical dream that is only a faint hope that may someday be a possibility. Family meal times are a rare occurrence, but usually consist of fast food grabbed on the run and consumed by the kids in the back seat of the car enroute to some important calamity.

Oh, sidebar comment: Mom and Dad are having issues in their marriage and are under financial pressures. Duh! Yah think?

Who is permitting this turmoil in their lives? Who ultimately is causing this hectic lifestyle? What lifestyle are they demonstrating to their children? Good questions, but in reality it is the choice of our happy couple to continue on this path. Only they have the ability to say "yes" or "no" and make the decision to change.

A phrase to think about while you read this chapter: "CHANGE BEGINS WITH THE PERSON LOOKING BACK AT ME FROM MY MIRROR."

Most North American adults know how to drive a car. Next time you are sitting behind the wheel take a look at your feet.

If you are driving an Automatic, you will notice that there are a couple of pedals. The driver can only use one pedal at a time, and usually only one foot, the right foot, is engaged in the proper operation of the pedals. Some try to use both feet and use both pedals at the same time. Not a great idea!

Many cars (Standards) have three pedals on the floor, and these require both feet. The left foot is supposed to work the clutch, and this pedal is designed to allow us to coast and take a break from the journey, or, more commonly, to change gears. The middle pedal is the brake and this is designed to be used by the right foot to cause us to slow down or stop. What is even better: if we are braking, we cannot keep the same right foot on the gas pedal for acceleration. The driver will get into some real conflict and eventually have a wreck if he continues to try and run the car full-out all day, and working all of the pedals at the same time. This isn't rocket science, but why do many of us try and drive our lives this way? You have control over your pedals and you must take control for the consequences caused by their correct or incorrect operation. Only the driver can decide which pedal to engage while driving.

Is this what God intended—lives out of control and little or no time set aside to just be with God? God designed us to take charge of our time, and set aside time to rest and spend with him. If we only take time to spend with God when the opportunity arises, or when disaster strikes, then it will never happen. Even God decided to take his foot off the gas and have some rest. Are you able to keep up a pace that is faster than God's?

> 1 *"Thus the heavens and the earth, and all the host of them, were finished.* 2 *And on the seventh day God ended His work which He had done, and He rested on the seventh day from all His work which He had done.* 3 *Then God blessed the*

> *seventh day and sanctified it, because in it He rested from all His work which God had created and made"* (Genesis 2:1-3 NKJV).

Without some structure to your life you can only expect a random series of events each day. The above scenario makes me tired just writing it. Can you imagine *living* it? But in the end, who must take responsibility? Look in the mirror to see the only person that can initiate a change. At some point in our lives we all must take responsibility for our actions, and lack of discipline for every aspect of our lives—the least not being our spiritual condition and our attitude towards Church. Now to tie this all in with the topic of this book—EXITS.

It is easy to pin the whole Church Exit syndrome on the pastors and the Church leaders. They may be part of the problem, but it is not a reason for us personally to be let off the hook. Another excuse you may have heard is that we need to get back to the original "New Testament Church" model. Sounds cool, but do we really know what that looks like? This statement gives the illusion to those listening that the speaker has a real grip on what the real Church is all about. To make that statement, the speaker must have great spiritual insight on the revival in Acts.

Consequently, we are faced with a continuous flow of new Church organizational charts. Big Church needs to be small, small Church needs to be large, structured Church needs to be unstructured. Judging by the books and the chatter, the answer seems to be that your Church needs some new structure other than what the current structure is. Now that sounds easy to achieve! Guess what! The early New Testament Church had problems as well.

Taken from the Church program handed out in AD 95. I think the book is called Revelation and it details seven Churches and their strengths and weaknesses. Yes, the Church had flaws even then.

- ✓ Join our Church. The emperor is running low on martyrs.
- ✓ Join our Church and lose your job and have your property confiscated.
- ✓ Immorality is becoming an issue but we will overcome.
- ✓ Lots of our teachers are causing division, but we'll hold together.

Run that ad on the media and I bet you will see huge Church growth. That was the real deal for the New Testament Church. So you still think we must get back to this?

> [2] *My brethren, count it all joy when you fall into various trials,* [3] *knowing that the testing of your faith produces patience.* [4] *But let patience have its perfect work, that you may be perfect and complete, lacking nothing.* [5] *If any of you lacks wisdom, let him ask of God, who gives to all liberally and without reproach, and it will be given to him.* [6] *But let him ask in faith, with no doubting, for he who doubts is like a wave of the sea driven and tossed by the wind.* [7] *For let not that man suppose that he will receive anything from the Lord;* [8] ***he is a double-minded man, unstable in all his ways***" (James 1:2-8 NKJV).

Now this is a great thought: *"Count it all joy when you fall into various trials."* Yes, I have found that life is not perfect and we do not live in a perfect world. Stuff happens, as the expression goes. There is good news available, however. The good news is, to use a legal expression, that we can take steps and precautions to mitigate our damages.

I love sitting by the sea and watching the waves pound in from the Pacific. On the west coast of British Columbia is an area that has become a tourist attraction for storm watchers. Yes, some people actually find pleasure in watching storms. Vancouver Island, British Columbia, is world famous for its great winter storm watching and there is no better place to watch these storms than at Pacific Rim National Park, right on a cliff overlooking the rugged Pacific coastline. Winter storm watching is best experienced from the comfort and luxury of your ocean-view room. Witness nature's fury in all its glory right before your eyes. Cuddle up in front of your own fireplace or on your private deck and watch 50-foot waves endlessly pound the rugged rocky coast. Or sit in front of a huge stone fireplace in the Great Room while the storm rages outside the wall of windows. It is truly an amazing experience!

As the travel brochures say, yes, it is a truly amazing experience. It is amazing watching a storm at sea from the safety of land, but it is not so much fun experiencing a storm while at sea. A word that comes to mind is "terrifying." Been there and done that! Do I see a hint of green in your cheeks?

God has provided us an opportunity for shelter from these stormy experiences. Why not pull into a harbor once in a while, and get off the stormy sea? Try it, you will like it! I think it is called the "Normal Church." James 1:2-8 appears to be a pretty easy scripture to interpret. No great hidden theology here. Double-minded means to be not of a single mind—in other words, a person who cannot make a decision or establish a plan and then stick to it.

A double-minded person is fractured in their decision-making process, always changing their mind and direction, and basically working without a safety net. This means little or no structure or sense of direction. Even after a double-minded person does finally make a decision it is always "subject to change." Double-minded people like to second guess their decisions, or do not make a decision at all. They are the type of person who wants to be free-spirited and keep their options open at all times. "Impulsive" and "spontaneous" are terms that they love to apply to themselves. Sounds great, but the outcome is usually frustration, confusion, and stress in their lives. If life is just left to unfold on its own, it usually doesn't unfold but it can be expected to crash. James goes on to further summarize the outcome of a random life. His statement, "*he is a double-minded man, unstable in all his ways,*" just about says it all.

You have choices but only **you** can make the choice of what is best for **you** and your family. If you don't choose to take charge of your life, nobody can do it for you. A good place to start would be to take time off at the end of the week to recharge your batteries and get refocused for the coming week. Sunday is a great time to shut things down and take a break, go to Church, visit some friends, and perhaps have lunch together. Just take your foot off the gas for a while and see what a change it will make. It is your choice and it takes planning and the desire to stick to your plan to get closer to God, your family, and friends. Hebrews gives us a good tip about what we should be doing at Church.

24 *"And let us consider one another in order to stir up love and good works,* 25 *not forsaking the assembling of ourselves together, as is the manner of some, but exhorting one another, and so much the more as you see the Day approaching"* (Hebrews 10:24-25 NKJV).

A real challenge for Church and for families is looming on the horizon. If we do not focus on our spiritual health and our Church, then in about twenty years we will not recognize the Church of the Western culture. Church is already vastly different and marginalized compared to even a few years ago. Christians young and old are making a decision that other things are more important than Church. You have a choice. Make a decision to not go to Church, or make a decision to go to Church. It's a decision that only you can make.

Parents, by deciding not to attend Church, are not teaching their children the habit of attending Church. Yes, we are creatures of habit. Church should be one of those habits. The idea of Sunday being a time of worship and rest is quickly falling behind in many Christian families. If Church is not important for mom and dad, then how can we expect Church to have value in the lives of our kids and grand kids?

Oh, by the way: NEWS FLASH! If you have raised your family, and have reached the Freedom 55 plateau, you are probably now a grandparent. What is your attitude and ***consistent*** attendance at Church teaching your adult kids, and their kids (also known as your grandkids)? Did I say "consistent"?

Another sidebar comment: What do you talk about in front of your kids and grandkids? Are you current enough with the good things that God is doing today, or are you preoccupied with talking about the days of the dinosaurs in your past" "Those were the good old days at ABC Church when God was so real." You know the drill. Not everything that God is doing today needs to be a miracle or some huge revival experience. How about just the good things in the family of God?

Oh yeah, the other gripping subject that is sure to motivate your kids and grandkids. Many grandparents are so out of touch with today that they can only focus on the end time. It goes something like this, "We are in the end times, things are looking pretty bad, can't get any worse." Depress the life out of your kids and grandkids and this for sure will depress and scare them back to Church. Good grief! There is more to what God is doing today, so why not get in touch? Oh, that venting felt so good!

Church has taken a back seat to a lot of other seemingly important interests. In many cases, these other important interests are taking the place of Church and only adding more wood to the already-blazing fires of our crazy lives.

Now this brings us back to a previous chapter on what is normal for Church. Church is meant to be a house of prayer and worship where Christians gather together. Church is quickly becoming an event that may sometimes fit in our week—provided we can find enough time. There is getting to be less and less time, however, and so many Christians are not choosing Church. Each day still has 24 hours but we seem to figure that we don't have time. Perhaps we just need to have a plan for our time.

New styles and forms of Church are evolving in an attempt to try and fit in a few minutes of worship, evangelism, music, entertainment, and social networking. In some cases we have come to a point where we need to process people in under one hour and send them on their way. Get their Church pill, collect their donation, pump them up, and then out the door in under 60 minutes. We treat Church just like meal times for our frazzled mom and her kids at the opening of this chapter. Charge through some fast food outlet, jam a burger in the kids' mouths and we are good to go.

All churched out yet? Be careful! The pastor may be reading this.

A few years ago, Cherril and I were on a vacation trip, and we had been told by friends to make sure to attend this certain Church. It is one of the leading Churches in the particular area. (I have left out the location to prevent speculation.) We were told that the worship service was fantastic, and the music and speaking was top quality. This Church was on the cutting edge.

So we get to our destination city, we look at the Church section of the newspaper, and we locate the recommended Church's advertising. If this was today we would just Google the Church. This was before Google—a dinosaur story.

We welcome you to ABC Church.

Feel free to wear your boots, tennis shoes, sandals, or Crocs. Our services begin at either 9:00 a.m. or10:30 a.m. or noon. We respect your busy schedules by offering an opportunity for all to worship. We offer a written guarantee that the service will not extend past one hour. We encourage you to come and enjoy ABC Café which opens 30 minutes prior to each service. You can enjoy coffee, bagels, and donuts while mingling with friends…and making new ones.

The anticipated Sunday comes and we drive to the address given in the advertising. I dress for the occasion, wearing a brand new pair of Crocs as instructed in the ad.

Upon arrival at our destination we are greeted by the traffic people and directed to the "10:30 parking area." They have separate parking areas for each service in order to allow for a quick entry and departure from the services. It looks like things are happening. Those in the 9:00 a.m. parking area are already leaving. The traffic people are moving signs and barriers in preparation for the exit of the 9:00 a.m. lot. Very well organized!

We get parked, and the lot is filling quickly. We are instructed to proceed to the cafe area and the doors are open to the ABC Cafe. We get there, and the place is a beehive of activity. Starbucks has nothing on this place. Sales look to be brisk. The sound of the coffee machines blasting out coffees at only $3.00 per blast.

An announcement is made that the service will begin in 10 minutes. BAM! Right on cue, the electronic doors fly open and instructions are given to proceed to our seats.

To keep us entertained, an exceptional media production is playing on the screens giving us all the details of the Church programs that are coming up. We are told in the presentations that ABC Church is one of the fastest-growing and most progressive Churches in North America. They have programs that will meet every need.

At various times through the media presentation it is made clear to please move out of the sanctuary area as soon as the service has concluded. This speedy exit is required in order to consider the needs of those waiting to enter the next ***worship*** service. Pretty good organization and I would estimate about 800 people are pouring into the meeting area. The place is about two-thirds full. I guess we must have chosen an off day to attend. The Church appears to have seating for about 1,200. Very efficient traffic flow, as I notice the place is totally emptied out from the 9:00 a.m. group. When we enter, the entrances are well-served by the smiling people handing out literature.

We find our chosen seats and the band gets things going at precisely 10:20 a.m. They are playing some of the "expertly-arranged contemporary worship music" that we had been told to expect. No disappointment here with the warm up. The performance is exceptional.

The media presentation is now concluded, the band stops playing and the timer appears on the screens with the countdown for the service to start: 60 – 59 – 58 .... Zero – and bam! Just like magic the lights dim. The band fires up, the worship leaders hit the stage, and we are in full gear.

Right on queue, 10:30 a.m. on the dot.

Worshippers stand obediently as the band rocks out, the smoke machine belches and lights flash. Lyrics are projected on the screen, but almost no one sings them. The worship leaders are enthusiastic, and do a good job encouraging everyone to sing the songs on the screens. Seems like the crowd is enjoying the music. Few are singing, however, and a few have their hands raised as instructed.

To signal the end of worship, at 10:45 a.m., the lights come on, bright setting. The worship enhancement setting is put on fade. We are given a very compelling 10-minute presentation on the privilege of worshiping with our giving. We are assured that God will richly bless us for our generous donation to the offering and the supporting scriptures are quoted. The total time for the offering is about 10 minutes. Time now is 10:55 a.m. Better kick it up a notch if we are going to be out of here by 11:30 a.m.

Right after the offering, a sports figure is introduced and he speaks a locker room pep talk for a few minutes. Gets the enthusiasm built up pretty good for what is in store for us. Time now is 11:05 a.m.

Once again, exactly on schedule, the pastor walks on stage with a game show style of presentation. The crowd goes nuts and now for the happy time, the make-a-friend part of the service. We are encouraged to greet people, make them feel welcome and show them how friendly a place this is. We are now at 11:10 a.m. I forget to write down the name of my new best friend who assured me I was welcome. I don't think he asked me my name either, or the fact that I was a foreigner from Canada. I get over the disappointment.

The pastor delivers a very compelling sermon on some topic. At precisely 11:29 a.m. the timer comes on the overhead and counts down 60 – 59 – 58 ...... Zero – and bam! Just like magic the sermon ends and the lights hit full intensity. The bank of doors on the left side of the building fly open automatically. The advertising on the media screens, with a very radio-like voice, encourages us to exit the area in order to make room for the next service and, oh yes, plan to attend next Sunday.

Wow! We all feel blessed. The friendly Church has kept its written guarantee to have us in and out for our dose of Church in 60 minutes. Very impressive!

What is even more impressive is the fact that the Church claims to have a membership of about 5,000 people. Judging by the count I estimate that they can process about 4,000 people per Sunday. I guess the Sunday that we chose to attend was an off day. As I say, impressive.

We follow the crowd around the appointed walkways to our car. Once we all get in the car we come up with the common thought: "What just happened?" We also notice that very few if any people are actually standing around talking or visiting after the meeting.

I am exhausted just writing down this account of our Church experience that Sunday. I am sure you are exhausted just trying to read my account. You think I made this piece up, right? Not so. This is a true story. As I indicated earlier, this is a well-known Church that is used as a textbook example of how to achieve Church growth. My only question is, "Growth at what expense?" Does this achieve growth in numbers only? The system works well if the goal is to process a lot of people on Sunday morning. But the goal must be to do more than process people if they are to remain.

Now, by contrast read this quote from Jesus: [28]*"Come to Me, all you who labor and are heavy laden, and I will give you rest.* [29]*Take My yoke upon you and learn from Me, for I am gentle and lowly in heart, and you will find rest for your souls.* [30]*For My yoke is easy and My burden is light"* (Matthew 11:28-30 NKJV).

Jesus tells us that if we are weary of the religious exercises we are chasing then come to him for rest. Perhaps the reason we hear the expression "all churched-out" is that Christians are looking for more than just Church growth, but would like to perhaps obtain spiritual growth. Spiritual growth is not just achieved by attending the right Church and hearing the right sermon. Responsibility for growth is also in the hands of the believer. Feeding yourself the Word of God is a personal choice that is your responsibility. But the Church environment is a very key part of growth as well.

I think that the example that we just read about is the extreme but many Churches are not far behind this particular model. In an attempt to increase attendance, various models have been developed to keep the people coming in the doors. As we look around, however, we also find an alarming number of people hitting the Exits as well with the thought, "What just happened?"

Why do these models based on attendance continue to be rolled out? We, from the ordinary Church members all the way up to the senior pastor, find ourselves on an endless treadmill to achieve Church growth. The ordinary Christian cannot find time or the desire to attend Church so new models are designed to fit in with this marketing trend. Do everything in our power to get them in the doors and promise them in writing that it is only for 60 minutes. We can't get an offering if they don't attend.

The Church leaders feel pressured to do something to turn this bus around. The focus then comes on new programs and styles in order to try and boost Church attendance. Everything has been tried from Drive In Church, to Fast Food Church, to No Structure Church. I am sure the design department has the next model already on the drawing boards. In an ever-increasing need and pressure to keep the numbers and the resulting finances growing, various styles are adopted. Yes, finances play a big role in this drama. To run what we feel are the required programs for a successful Church, takes money. Modern-day Church is expensive. Is this really what Church is all about? Be honest with yourself, now!

CHANGE BEGINS WITH THE PERSON LOOKING BACK AT ME FROM MY MIRROR.

Lack of commitment and the inability to make a decision and then stick to it is a real fact of life. This problem is becoming a lifestyle for our society. As Christians, the Elephant in the Room is that we as the Church are facilitating this problem. Christians are inviting and welcoming this spirit to enter our Churches. It is no longer sufficient to moan and groan about Church and reflect on the way it used to be or what it should be. If we do not want to lose what God intends his Church to be then it is up to Christians to look in the mirror and initiate change. It is always easy to blow holes in a family, but it takes a lot more effort to restore or revive a family that is suffering.

What are you going to do about it? Are you going to continue to float until we look back at this point in time, and say, "Those were the good old days, but I don't recognize Church any longer"? It may be coming sooner than you think. What are we going to do about it?

Man up and make the decision to change back to normal Church. Just make a decision and stick to it. Try something that may be a huge step for you. Speak to your pastor and tell him that you have decided to make the decision to change and add stability to your life and your attitude. Encourage him that you are praying that the Lord will give him the direction and courage to also bring change and stability back to your Church.

Two conflicting words appear to be used in this comment—change and stability. How can this be the case? To find stability we need to revive the ability to make some personal decisions that will require us to change our attitudes. Pray that the foundations will be rebuilt and return to what the "Normal Church" is meant to be. Take the pressure off your pastor. The goal will be Church health which will produce Church growth. There is much more to growth than just numbers and finances. Remember the chapter on raising sheep. Healthy sheep will produce an abundance of lambs. As one of the sheep, what can you do? Pray about it, and make a decision. What can you do to bring about change to become a healthy Church?

A law of physics for pastors and Church leaders. Newton's Third Law: **For every action, there is an equal and opposite reaction.** This isn't exactly rocket science, even though it is a rule of physics.

The statement means that in every interaction, there is a pair of forces acting on the two interacting objects. The size of the force on the first object equals the size of the force on the second object. The direction of the force on the first object is opposite to the direction of the force on the second object. Forces always come in pairs—equal and opposite action-reaction.

You have most likely seen the demonstration of this fact using Newton's Cradle. This is more than a toy, as it shows this principle extremely well.

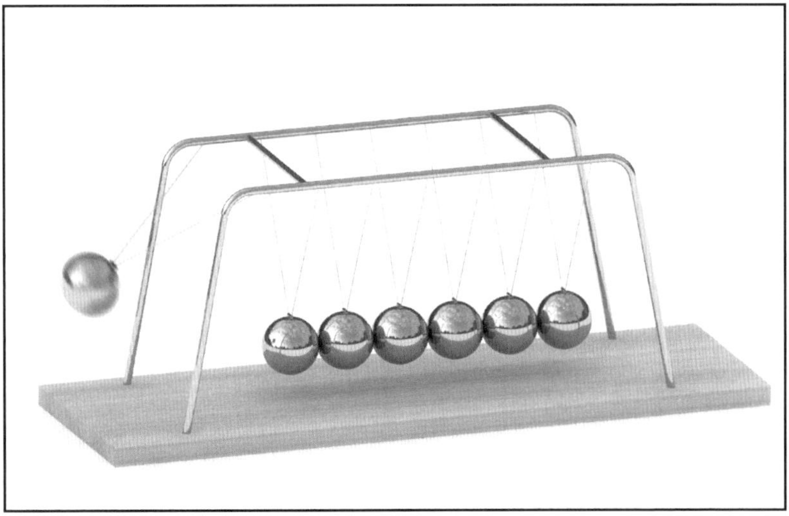

The device consists of seven steel balls suspended on pieces of thin fish line. Take the ball on the left side, pull it to the left about three inches, and let it go. Amazing, but the ball on the right side will also move about three inches to the right when the left ball impacts with it and the remaining six balls. You can go to YouTube and type in "Newton's Cradle Demonstration" to see a demonstration.

Now consider that each individual person in your congregation is represented by a steel ball. Have you ever heard the expression that no man is an island? Take any group of people and when you pay attention you will see how the dynamics of this statement really works. When you consider that Jesus compares a Church to a body all joined together and working together (Ephesians 4:1-16), then you can really see how the example of Newton's Cradle is at work in a Church. Without careful consideration, the unsettling experiences of one person can affect a whole circle of people who are connected to that person.

For some reason, this principle appears to be ignored in many Churches. Leadership decides that it should grow some particular program or add some new staff, and neither the existing staff nor the members of the congregation are included in any of the plans leading up to this change. One of the balls is now put in motion in Newton's Cradle, without warning, and a whole series of events is set in motion. It seems so difficult for information to be communicated. Must be that the ordinary folk aren't able to comprehend these large executive decisions. So without careful thought, planning, and consultation a new direction and a department is created.

OOPS! Leadership has decided to take a new course of direction. The decision is made to cut some people, some programs, or some department. How is it that the department and people that were so important last year are no longer needed this year? Leadership doesn't consider it important that there be any consultation or information. The rest of the body is expected to just adapt in the dark. A great shock wave is felt as one the balls in Newton's Cradle is once again placed in motion, and people begin moving toward the Exits, little by little.

These dynamics are not exclusive to Churches, but my point is: with just a bit more care, prayer, and advice much of the fallout can be prevented or at least mitigated. It is obvious that changes must be made in any body. We do not live in a static world. But unless the organization is only made up of one person and is doing nothing that is interactive with people, it can't continually make unilateral decisions. Not many of those types of organizations exist for very long.

With a little bit of care we can reduce the amount of friction within our Churches. Refer back to the chapter on the vineyard again. In our sample winery we saw great planning and stability. Consider many successful businesses and you will see that stability of the employees is a common denominator. I have some friends and associates who are managing some pretty significant businesses. Without exception, one of their strong points is their ability to attract good people and experience very little turnover. In fact, when you are talking to these successful leaders they will tell you one of their keys to success. "We have very little turnover of staff. Many have been employed here for years." Stability in a Church body is also key for the Church's health—for workers, and for the sheep. See if some of these points would also assist your Church to experience better health.

Church Health: If the staff and volunteers are stable, leadership can invest its energy in moving the Church body forward. Leaders will not be distracted by the need to continually hire new replacement employees. They won't be required to staff their human resources department to feed the revolving door.

Church Staff: With a stable workforce, staff and volunteers are surrounded by co-workers who know their jobs, know each other, and know what they're all striving to do together as a Church body. They're able to focus on productivity and service instead of continually teaching new people how to fulfill their responsibilities. Training and development can be invested in helping dedicated staff and volunteers, helping them to grow and improve, rather than aimed at constantly rebuilding foundational skills in an ever-changing workforce.

If the Church has unstable staff and volunteers then the sheep are thrown off-balance by that nagging feeling that the leadership of the Church is not on their game. When a feeling of insecurity rises up within the Church then people begin nervously eyeing the Exit. May be just a trickle but any leak is a bad leak if left long enough. When one of the sheep leaves, this can have much greater consequences than a customer leaving a business.

Volunteers: With a drive towards meeting the needs of the Church efficiently and effectively, volunteers like to know who they're dealing with and what the focus of their Church is. Volunteers should *not* be made to feel that their purpose is to support the staff, but the staff are to support the volunteers. Better still, nobody is supporting anybody; they are all working together as a team. Good communication increases team-building.

A Church does not have customers but we have people who we serve who are even more important than a business customer. We have sheep and new lambs. Much of the work in a Church can and should be performed by volunteers who have hands-on contact with the sheep. A very simple fact: staff are tending the sheep because they are paid. Stop the pay and the staff members are gone. It may hurt to hear this, but it is a true statement. You know it is. Pastors and staff may come and go, but the volunteers of the Church hopefully remain. They themselves are sheep.

Ouch! It sounds like I am saying that all paid staff are 'hirelings.' No, I realize that pastors and church secretaries need to pay their rent and buy groceries too. This is true. Moreover, many roles that need to be performed in the Church may not be efficiently performed by volunteers alone. Both staff and volunteers are valuable. Again this depends on the heart conditions of each. I have been in board meetings when a pastor has made a comment such as, "I would rather have paid staff than volunteers. You have more control over a paid staff member than an unpaid volunteer." Both attitudes are equally incorrect. Does this clarify my comment?

What is really needed are "good people with the success of the ministry on their heart." The key is the right people for the right job and with the right motive to be engaged in the Church. This is regardless of their status—paid or volunteer. We need both. Volunteers respect the staff, the staff respect the volunteers, and without question the staff respect other staff. (Great thought, but sometimes a difficult ideal to achieve.) But my point is: neither a volunteer or a staff member is more important than the other.

It is a truth, however, that a lot of productive work can be completed by a dedicated volunteer who is working out of a heartfelt compulsion rather than out of a sense of duty. When a staff member has lost their passion for the ministry or is performing what is required simply to get their paycheck then it becomes an issue. No matter if it is in business or in church, a staff person only working for the paycheck is damaging. This is not good for the employee and is surely not good for the organization and those they serve.

Even more damaging is when a staff member is moved down the "pecking order" to the dark zone. In what can only be described as "internal shunning," meetings with other staff are discouraged or impeded either in a display of power or in an effort to destroy moral so that a dismissal is not required but a resignation is forthcoming. Does this ring any bells, Church?

I have decided to not avoid this issue because I want to bring out the value of both staff and volunteers working together in harmony. To say that pastors and church staff are not of value is not my intent. To say that volunteers are less valuable because they are more difficult to control is also not correct. Far from it! It would be equally wrong to state that volunteers are not of any value because they don't cost us anything. These important parts of the body do have great value. Without question! (See 2 Corinthians 8:1-7). It does raise the idea, however, that both groups, the staff and the volunteers, need to give careful consideration to the fact that the others are also an integral part of the body and have value.

What are the sheep's expectations and needs? What background do the sheep have? Often staff and volunteers depend on standardized procedures and productive relationships that assure open communication with minimal hassle. Workforce instability at a sheepfold dampens those relationships and anticipated performance. This confusion draws valuable resources to repeatedly rebuild connections and understandings.

Investors (Tithers and faithful Givers): Increasingly, savvy givers monitor workforce stability. Their Church is where they invest—or consider investing. Stability is vital to them. They want to know that the Church body will be able to produce to improve shareholder value. (Translation: they don't want to give to a Church that doesn't make good use of their money.) Constantly pumping resources into recruitment, training, and rebuilding efficiencies defeats expansion, growth, and even the Church's efforts to maintain the status quo. If faithful givers are leery of putting money into a Church that will not make the highest and best use of that capital then those givers move elsewhere. The giving does not dry up; the mouse is simply clicked and the money is diverted elsewhere.

Pastors, believe what you may. It makes no difference whether you think this is right or wrong. It is a fact for the average guy sitting in your congregation.

The Church Operations: Recruiting new workers into a Church is essential for the continued health of all Churches in the field. Workers and volunteers usually look for career paths that show promise of personal and professional growth, expanding opportunity, and dependable employment with good working conditions and rewards. Rampant instability may send loud signals that this career path is not a wise decision and qualified workers will seek other alternatives. Each of these efforts draws resources away from endeavors that can strengthen the Church's goal to serve. With continual turnover, resources are drained and then heavy recruitment becomes a mandate instead of an option. I have often heard from those who have worked in Churches that their employment was very stressful and a source of bewilderment. What is wrong with this picture? Once these former Church workers have left the employ of the Church and entered the outside work force, they make comments such as, "The business world can produce settled and content working environments, but why is the Church in constant turmoil?"

Economy at Large: Staff and volunteer instability creates an unstable marketplace in a community. Word travels fast to similar Churches that a particular Church is having stability issues. Result? Church resources are directed toward stabilizing, backfilling, and maintaining, rather than the health and welfare of the sheep. The expansion of local and foreign mission projects and the local presence of the Church in its community is inhibited. Growth is restricted by a sort of paranoia that ties together the feet of resources that could be running into a stronger future. Progress becomes considerably slowed, diminishing enthusiasm for giving of offerings. Givers lose their inspiration to give and the drive that creates greater growth opportunities for Church health is reduced. It's all connected.

CHANGE BEGINS WITH THE PERSON LOOKING BACK AT ME FROM MY MIRROR.

- ✓ Constant change creates constant stress.
- ✓ Staff changes damage the sheep. Bonds have been built and when this bond is broken some are injured in the process.
- ✓ Every person has a sphere of influence. Move one person within the sphere and it affects many people. When one person is removed, then a number of connected people are soon to follow.

EXIT 13

FLAWS

My daughter-in-law, Shara, and my four-year-old granddaughter, Clara, pulled up to a busy intersection. While waiting at the red light, from her rear-view mirror, Shara noticed Clara staring intently at a very overweight woman walking her very small dog across the street. From the backseat Clara exclaimed, "That's weird!" As Shara braced for the possible worst, Clara gleefully expressed, "That lady's dog is too small for her!"

As Christians, what do we see in people? And even more important, what do we see in other Christians? Do we focus on the positive or do we focus on the negative and then quickly point out these flaws? Just like Clara, we can choose to see what we wish to see.

> [1] *"Judge not, that you be not judged.* [2] *For with what judgment you judge, you will be judged; and with the measure you use, it will be measured back to you.* [3] *And why do you look at the speck in your brother's eye, but do not consider the plank in your own eye?* [4] *Or how can you say to your brother, 'Let me remove the speck from your eye'; and look, a plank is in your own eye?* [5] *Hypocrite! First remove the plank from your own*

eye, and then you will see clearly to remove the speck from your brother's eye" (Matthew 7:1-5 NKJV).

Jesus is making some points worth paying attention to:

✓ Don't judge people unless you are prepared to be judged.

✓ The same measuring cup that you use to judge people will be the measuring cup that will be used to judge you. With some of us, I don't think we use measuring cups. A pail comes to mind.

✓ Perhaps you could see better if you took the plank out of your own eye. Did you know that those with planks in their eyes are called hypocrites? (Note the exclamation mark in the verse.)

Is this you, or is this me, being described in these words by Jesus?

A number of years ago I developed an interest in a hobby of buying and selling diamonds. This led to taking a course with the Gemological Institute of America (the GIA course). I thought that if I was going to trade diamonds, it would be a good idea to learn something about diamonds.

Hey, ladies, I bet you didn't know that *most* diamonds have flaws. In fact, it is the flaws in the diamond that are one of the first things to look for to see if it is, in fact, a real diamond. The correct term for these flaws is "inclusions." There are four things you look for in a diamond to judge its quality and value. These are referred to as the four C's, and they are: Cut - Clarity - Carat - Color.

One of the first things you check to see if a diamond is real is to take a 10-power microscope or a 10-power jeweler's loupe and carefully look for inclusions. It is very hard to manufacture a fake stone that will contain inclusions. If you see an inclusion, this gives you the first clue that the diamond may be real. There *are* flawless diamonds, but they are quite rare. Not many ladies will be wearing flawless diamonds. They are more rare and more costly and not within the budget of many a young man. Most ladies accepting the ring of great sentimental value don't care. The flaw she has in her stone will only remind her father about the guy she is about to marry.

With the progress in technology, the fake diamond makers have come up with ways to fix this defect of perfection in fake stones. Yes, in the fake diamond business, perfection is actually a defect. CVD-grown synthetic diamonds have become more abundant in the gem market and they even have inclusions. This makes it harder now to tell a fake from the real thing. To separate the fakes from the genuine has now become more difficult, but not impossible.

To be a good judge of diamond quality you do not spend a lot of time studying the fakes. You must spend a lot of time studying the real deal, the real diamonds—some with inclusions and some without. You must know the perfect diamond very well and study perfect diamonds. A diamond grader who is studying real diamonds every day will have less trouble identifying a fake when he sees one. He is not spending his days looking for fakes, he is spending his days looking at the real thing and he will spot the occasional fake that comes across his path.

Spend time looking at Jesus; he is the flawless diamond to use as the pattern. Luke 20:39 is an interesting scripture where we see the religious leaders of the day checking out Jesus very carefully to see if he was a fake or not. They could not find a flaw in Jesus and they summed up their inspection this way: [39] *"Then some of the scribes answered and said, 'Teacher, You have spoken well.'* [40] *But after that they dared not question Him anymore"* (Luke 20:39-40 NKJV).

Perhaps we should learn to do the same. Focus on Jesus and not on the potential fakes. Study scripture for yourself. If you saturate yourself in the pure word of God then you will be able to pick out the genetically modified doctrines. Be aware that there are fakes, but don't spend a lot of time looking for the fakes and pointing them out to your friends and family. This will only mar the pleasure of the perfect diamond that you do have.

The salvation of Jesus makes you personally perfect in the eyes of God. Don't take the engagement ring that you gave your wife when you were young and broke and point out the inclusions to her.

Just as with diamonds you can use this simple test to tell if people are fake or not: compare them with the real stone—Jesus. If others who are reading this do the same, then don't forget you will also be compared to Jesus. Will you come up fake or real? I am sure you have met people who like to appear as if they have a handle on truth and are quick to point out the inclusions in other Christians. By drawing the attention to the inclusions in another Christian they are able to deflect attention from the flaws of their own lives. They are attempting to appear perfect and all-knowing of spiritual things. Perhaps those who continually point out the apparent flaws in others have a pride issue of their own, and attempt to impress others by their great knowledge of the scriptures. Just a thought.

With Google and email it is now even easier to point out the inclusions of others to make oneself appear more spiritual and flawless. I am speaking from firsthand experience. In writing this book I have been talking to and emailing a number of these people.

The range of comments has been wide. Everything from positive testimonies to the insistence that President Obama is a Muslim. This is apparently something that I should be made aware of. Somehow I will be a better Christian with this great insight that only my advisor knows. I don't know the president and, in fact, I am not an American. I am Canadian. How does this news flash make me a better Christian?

It seems like the flavor of the month is currently on drawing attention to the leaders of certain ministries who have written books or appear on TV. I have received emails drawing my attention to the inclusions that may be present in these personalities. It apparently is crucial that I should know about them. The wisdom of those giving me this information is great and I am sure I will be a better Christian with this knowledge. Yes, I also think that some of the personalities who have been brought to my attention are nuts. But there is no need for me to focus on this.

I have a weird side in my personality. In some ways I am actually anticipating the mail, phone calls and emails that I most likely will receive once this book gets into circulation. I am sure my flaws will be clearly drawn to my attention. I am sure that you will find out that I do have a few. If some find that my flaws are significant then in fact you may find me on the internet. Oh well. The price I must pay for being human and flawed. Good news is, however, that I am a son of God and he paid the price for my flaws.

A new growth industry has developed. There are numerous web sites devoted to pointing out the errors of others whom I don't even know. In fact, some I haven't heard of. Google "False Prophets on TV." Wow! Mind numbing. Some are good and some are bad, as reported by a certain web site. Look at another web site and it is giving the message to be careful of the website that is telling you the bad guy is really a good guy. So what? I need to keep my eyes on Jesus and see what I can do to change my image in the mirror each morning and become a better reflection of Jesus. Don't you think that would be more productive to a world in sin that needs change? Oh, by the way, I have been told to be cautious of lady teachers.

My goal as a Christian is not to be a reflection of some personality. My goal should be to be a reflection of Jesus. This is not much different from testing to see if a diamond is real or fake. You don't compare the diamond to a fake diamond. You always compare the diamond being tested to a real diamond. If the attributes of a particular diamond are the same as the real sample diamond, then you can conclude that the diamond is genuine. Therefore don't compare others to you and me. If you do conclude that some book or teaching contains a false doctrine then exercise your choice to put it down and forget about it.

Previously, I mentioned a man living in Turkey who experienced a miraculous conversion from Islam to Christianity. In my estimation, he is a true follower of Jesus. In 1980 there were about 40 Christians in Turkey. That's not a typo; there were 40 Christians in the country of Turkey. In 1988 this man became a Christian by no other means than reading a copy of the NIV Bible. When it was discovered that he had become a Christian he was subjected to 10 days of torture in an attempt to get him turned around and "back on track" as a Muslim. He refused to deny Jesus. He is now the founder and pastor of one of the Churches in the Book of Revelation, the seventh Church, the Church of Smyrna—but 2,000 years later. In his testimony he said that the more he was tortured the stronger his faith became to endure the pain. He kept his eyes on his new and perfect diamond, Jesus. That was in 1988 and even after the pain and torture he is still walking as a disciple of Jesus, even in Turkey, a Muslim country.

Not just in Turkey, but in many countries around the world, Christians are being persecuted for their faith in Jesus. A good friend of ours is a spokesman for the Persecuted Church and is informing Canadian Christians about persecution today. Persecution is ongoing in 54 countries around the world today. Believers are beaten and put in prison and even killed. In fact, 480 believers are killed every day for their faith in Christ. One dies every three-and-a-half minutes. We in the West can help these believers by not forgetting them and by praying for them.

In the big picture of the global Christian Church, do all these important news tips pointing out the potential fakes have any importance—which evangelist is good and which one is not really on track? Perhaps just check out the plank in your own eye. We are not followers of evangelists, presidents, or authors. We are to be followers of Jesus. Stick to the Word of God.

In a previous chapter I asked a question about the Normal Christian Church. This account is from the "Normal" Church in Smyrna. The number of true Christians has apparently grown from 40 in 1980 (*not a typo*) to about 120,000 as reported in a recent article. This is a small number compared to the total population of Turkey—79,749,461 (July 2012 est.), but it is phenomenal church growth nevertheless. Important fact: the Prime Minister of Turkey is a Muslim. Does this change anything?

Now you be the judge. Provide this news flash to these people being persecuted around the world for their faith: "Some evangelist I don't agree with may be spreading a false doctrine in the States someplace." Do you think it would have changed things for the 480 believers who are killed each day for their faith? Even more ridiculous would be to supply them with information of great importance that "Muslims are not Christians." That is a no-brainer in Turkey! This is almost as big a news flash as my granddaughter's statement: "Mommy, that lady's dog is too small." Yes, it was perhaps a flaw, but so what? We cannot impose Christianity on an ungodly world. We can only demonstrate the reflection of Jesus.

There will always be someone spreading what might possibly be false doctrine some place. This was even the case in the early Church. Be careful of this but don't get so bogged down with it that it affects your ability to soak up the real truth that Jesus has for you personally. People are attracted to Jesus by the gospel that you spread by both deed and word. Don't taint your testimony by being on a constant downer about some other guy some place. Stick to the pure Word yourself and let God take care of the other guy someplace.

As "great and knowledgeable" Christians perhaps we should look into the doctrinal views of the tortured men and women. We should make sure that they agree with our particular slant on things. How could these tortured and slaughtered Christians possibly be theologically sound if they have a different doctrine than ours? I am sure that being post-Trib or pre-Trib is not that significant while you are being tortured for your faith in Jesus. Come to think of it, sounds like they are currently living in the middle of the Tribulation. Does this hit a nerve and sound all too familiar for some in our Churches?

We recently visited a Church while on vacation. The main thing that I recall about the Sunday morning sermon was the number of evangelists that the preacher was tearing up by shining light on their flaws. Not being an American, I hadn't even heard of some of the names being dropped. When we left the service we felt rejuvenated now that we had been enlightened about the alleged false teachers. The pastor must have been a real spiritual giant to have found all of that information on Google. I am sure he didn't personally know any of the characters he was ripping up.

Think about your actions next time you decide to focus on some fake diamonds. You may be shocked. They could actually be real diamonds but just have inclusions. Even if they are fake, what good will that news do for the Christian that is receiving your great news? How about the non-Christians that hear your great news about the fake diamond? Does it make them want to rush out and embrace the real gospel message. Not likely! It will only confuse them because what assurance do they have in listening to you that you are *also* not a fake?

The title of this book, as you know by now, is EXITS. Don't be the one standing in the Exit holding the door open to assist others in the Church to leave. Our Churches have some suffering individuals who are going through their own form of torture. Just like our men and women in Turkey, they need encouragement to focus on the real diamond and not the fakes.

> 8 *"Finally, brethren, whatever things are true, whatever things are noble, whatever things are just, whatever things are pure, whatever things are lovely, whatever things are of good report, if there is any virtue and if there is anything praiseworthy—meditate on these things.* 9 *The things which you learned and received and heard and saw in me, these do, and the God of peace will be with you"* (Philippians 4:8-9 NKJV).

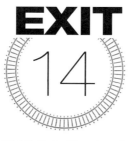

EXIT 14

OVERWHELMING!

Some can make the topic of doctrine so complex that you wonder what ever happened to the simplicity of the gospel. Others can make doctrine so basic and so loose that you wonder if it still contains the gospel message. And still others can lay out such a heavy warning that you are afraid to do anything and question everything. This leads to paranoia and robs you of the joy of your salvation. Many times the whole topic of doctrine is just overwhelming. So what is the answer for a simple guy just wanting to serve the Lord?

Of course, doctrine is important in the Christian Church. If it wasn't then we wouldn't be warned about false doctrine. If doctrine was not to be taught, then scripture would just tell us to forget about it. This is not the case. There are many scriptures that give us encouragement or warnings and teach us the importance of sound doctrine.

> *"...that we should no longer be children, tossed to and fro and carried about with every wind of doctrine, by the trickery of men, in the cunning craftiness of deceitful plotting"* (Ephesians 4:14 NKJV).

The wording of this passage tells us that doctrine can be as variable as the wind. If you just took what I said out of context, then you could have a real heyday with my words. The gossip will be that this chapter is pure heresy because I apparently am saying that doctrine is of no value. Not so! For sure there are those that come to kill and destroy your joy as a Christian with excessive doctrines. Yet others may lead you to believe that with the wrong doctrine you could actually lose your salvation. Already this topic is getting overwhelming.

Scripture is very clear that we are secure in Christ Jesus our Lord:

> [37] *"Yet in all these things we are more than conquerors through Him who loved us.* [38] *For I am persuaded that neither death nor life, nor angels nor principalities nor powers, nor things present nor things to come,* [39] *nor height nor depth, nor any other created thing, shall be able to separate us from the love of God which is in Christ Jesus our Lord"* (Romans 8:37-39 NKJV).

So, let's work on the premise that one set of instructions should apply to any time in history or the future, for any geographic location, denomination, or any Christian—whether just saved today or saved for many years. So what is the simplified answer regarding the topic of Christian doctrine? "Simple," you say? I have found it to be an overwhelming topic at times. The debates can become so heated over doctrine that you see Church splits and a polarization over the various points of view. Even worse, some in the Church just give up and you see a group heading for the Exits. How about those new Christians? They have little Bible knowledge to start with and suddenly they are embroiled in one of these great Church debates over who is right and who is wrong.

So what is basic Christian doctrine? A good definition could be: "Christianity is a faith founded on a message of good news rooted in the significance of the life, death, and resurrection of Jesus Christ." In scripture, doctrine refers to the entire body of essential theological truths that define and describe that message (Titus 1:9). The message includes historical facts, such as those regarding the events of the life of Jesus Christ. And New Testament teachings about Jesus are built on the foundation of the Old Testament. Another way to look at doctrine is that it is the foundation of our faith that makes us Christians and that is separate from other philosophies or religions.

Jesus gives us a caution about the teaching of doctrine:

> [3] *"Therefore whatever they tell you to observe, that observe and do, but do not do according to their works; for they say, and do not do.* [4] *For they bind heavy burdens, hard to bear, and lay them on men's shoulders; but they themselves will not move them with one of their fingers.* [5] *But all their works they do to be seen by men. They make their phylacteries broad and enlarge the borders of their garments"* (Matthew 23:3-5 NKJV).

Not complicated. This is very easy to understand. Some, under the banner of doctrine, will bind heavy burdens on you, and lay them on your shoulders. This helps them develop their large egos and stroke their own pride. Without question, doctrine is important, and we need to understand the basics of our faith. Beware of those that are using their so-called knowledge and use of doctrine to make themselves appear knowledgeable and have control over others.

To understand this statement, look at the definition of a "phylactery" from Matthew 23:5. Admit it. You never heard of it.

What is a "phylactery"? They are two small square leather boxes containing slips inscribed with scriptural passages and traditionally worn on the left arm and on the head by observant Jewish men, and especially adherents of Orthodox Judaism during morning weekday prayers.

Phylacteries can be bought in the gift shop for the spiritual big shot that has everything. If you had a big box of scriptures on your arm and stuck to your forehead, then people would assume that this guy is a real spiritual giant and a super star in the Church. Do you get the picture? They wore their knowledge of scripture as a status symbol. Be careful of these guys and pay attention to what Jesus also observed: *"For they bind heavy burdens, hard to bear, and lay them on men's shoulders."*

So how have I attempted to simplify this in my own life? Stay firm to the teaching of scripture and be a disciple of Jesus. At the same time, I don't wake up each morning all burdened down because some false prophet may jump out and steal my salvation and joy. I don't live in a bubble, so how do I encourage other Christians to grow and at the same time admonish them to stay clear of the weird zone?

To illustrate, do you remember the movie, *JAWS*, from many years ago (June 20, 1975)? JAWS? Wow! Most of you were not even born then! It was the story of this huge shark swimming around eating unwary swimmers. After a few weeks of this movie playing in the theaters you couldn't get anyone to go swimming. Not even in a swimming pool! Jaws might get them.

How about a more recent article in today's paper (June, 2013): "A fisherman in Belarus, who was hoping to get a photo with a beaver, was brutally attacked and later died. It was the most serious in a string of beaver attacks on humans in Belarus, as the rodents have turned increasingly aggressive." Watch out, city folks! When approaching any ponds be cautious of the presence of killer beavers!

We don't want doctrine to end up in the category of Christian paranoia that can rob us of our joy as a Christian. Yes, be cautious and understand the warnings of scripture, but focus on the clear truth.

SOME DOCTRINE IS CLEAR AND NON-NEGOTIABLE: Scripture is very clear on the key points that make us part of the family of God. It is not possible to be a Christian if you do not cling to the basic doctrine of salvation. This is not negotiable. This is the black and white doctrine—true or false. The Coles notes of becoming a Christian.

Perhaps you are not yet a Christian but have decided that you need the assurance that you are one of God's children. Perhaps you don't feel that you can live up to God's expectations and "keep all the rules." This illustration will demonstrate just how simple God's plan for your salvation is. At the expense of being a bit overdramatic, let's say you are at death's door and you need to have the assurance without a shadow of doubt that you will end up in the arms of Jesus. You don't have time to study all of the many doctrines and sift through the apparent rules. You may not have led a stellar life of exceptional purity. Even if you did, that is not enough to grant you a pardon when you stand before Almighty God.

There is great news, and this will only take a few seconds to master. This little road map is all that you need to help you navigate through scripture and receive Jesus as your personal Savior. With these simple steps you will be granted your adoption papers to become a "child of God."

Christian doctrine is built on this simple foundation.

This is your road map to eternal life. The price of admission has been paid in full.

1. God offers a wonderful plan for your life. He doesn't want any to be separated from his great love.

God's love: *"God so loved the world that He gave His one and only Son, that whoever believes in Him shall not perish, but have eternal life"* (John 3:16 NIV).

God's plan: (Christ speaking) ***"I have come that they may have life, and that they may have it more abundantly"*** (that it might be full and meaningful) (John 10:10 NKJV).

Most people are not experiencing the abundant life. Why? Because…

2. People are born into this world separated from God because of sin.

Therefore, they cannot know and experience God's love and plan for their life.

Humanity is sinful: *"All have sinned and fall short of the glory of God"* (Romans 3:23 NKJV). People were created to have fellowship with God; but, because of their stubborn self-will, they choose to go their own independent way, and fellowship with God is broken. This self-will, characterized by an attitude of active rebellion or passive indifference, is evidence of what the Bible calls sin.

God and humanity are separated: *"The wages of sin is death"* (spiritual separation from God) (Romans 6:23 NIV). God is holy and mankind is sinful. A great canyon separates the two. People are continually trying to reach God and the abundant life through their own efforts, such as a good life, philosophy, or religion—but they inevitably fail. There is only one way to bridge this canyon…

3. God will accept only one form of payment for humanity's sin. He bought your ticket. Jesus Christ paid it all. Through Jesus you can know and experience God's love and plan for your life.

Jesus died in our place: ***"God demonstrates His own love toward us, in that while we were yet sinners, Christ died for us"*** (Romans 5:8 NKJV).

He rose from the dead: ***"Christ died for our sins…He was buried…He rose again the third day…He was seen by Cephas, then by the twelve. After that He was seen by over five hundred…"*** (1 Corinthians 15:3-6 NKJV).

He is the only way to God: ***"Jesus said to him, 'I am the way and the truth and the life. No one comes to the Father, except through Me'"*** (John 14:6 NIV). God has bridged the canyon which separates us from him by sending his Son, Jesus Christ, to die on the cross in our place to pay the penalty for our sins.

It is not enough just to know these three conditions…

4. To accept Jesus Christ as your Savior is a personal choice. God is offering you his gift. Only you can receive it, however. The choice is yours. By your acceptance you can know and experience God's love and plan for your life.

We must receive Christ: ***"As many as received Him, to them He gave the right to become children of God, to those who believe in His name"*** (John 1:12 NKJV).

We receive Christ through faith: ***"By grace you have been saved through faith, and that not of yourselves; it is the gift of God, not of works, lest anyone should boast"*** (Ephesians 2:8-9 NKJV).

When we receive Christ, we experience a New Birth: (Read John 3:1-8.)

We receive Christ by personal invitation: (Christ speaking) ***"Behold, I stand at the door and knock. If any one hears My voice and opens the door, I will come in to him…"*** (Revelation 3:20 NKJV).

Receiving Christ involves turning to God from self. The term *repentance* means a true confession that you are a sinner. You are not able to make yourself pure. You are trusting Christ to come into your life to forgive your sins and to make you what He wants you to be. Just to agree intellectually that Jesus Christ is the Son of God and that he died on the cross for your sins is not enough. Nor is it enough to have an emotional experience. You receive Jesus Christ into your heart by faith, as an act of your will. Jesus has paid the price in full. The decision is now yours. Acceptance or rejection?

You now have the foundation of the complete Christian doctrine as published by Jesus. Now all you have to do is read the Bible for yourself and you will gather the building blocks to build a complete and full life with God. Now that you are a child of God, read his Word and you will grow.

A SUMMARY OF CHRISTIAN DOCTRINE.

1. There is only one God. God is the creator of the universe, including you. He is one God consisting of three characters. The Father, Son, and Holy Spirit are called the Trinity.
2. Jesus was born of a virgin. He was born of a woman but with no earthly father. His Father is God. The name Jesus means "God saves."
3. Jesus is the Son of God, part of God, and therefore he is God. Jesus came to earth for the sole purpose to live out the gospel message in a body of flesh and give us the opportunity to be saved.
4. Jesus was crucified and died in our place to give us forgiveness for our sins if we only believe. Everyone dies, so his dying was not enough. There is more.

5. Jesus rose again after three days in a tomb. Without Jesus rising from the dead, he would be nothing more than another holy man who died. Jesus conquered sin and death when he left the grave and came back to life.
6. Every person has a sin nature, and is born into this world already separated from God. This is why we have evil in this world. Natural humanity is born without God. Sin is the absence of God dwelling within us.
7. There is a hell, and this world is an evil place. Hell is the ultimate penalty after death for those who reject Jesus Christ. God does not send people to hell, but people choose to go to hell by rejecting Jesus. Without Jesus, everyone is destined for hell already.
8. Heaven is a real place. There is life after death. Heaven is the reward and final resting place for those who have accepted the salvation Jesus gives. By choice we can become joint-heirs with Jesus and have eternal life in heaven. He is standing at your door and knocking now. Will you let him in?
9. We are not alone on the earth. Because of the resurrection of Jesus, Christians can receive the Holy Spirit in our lives as our comforter. All Christians have the Holy Spirit living within them.
10. God has supplied a manual that gives us detailed instructions on how to avoid sin, and live in harmony with God and our fellow citizens. "*. . . the Holy Scriptures, which are able to make you wise for salvation through faith which is in Christ Jesus.* [16] *All Scripture is given by inspiration of God, and is profitable for doctrine, for reproof, for correction, for instruction in righteousness,* [17] *that the man of God may be complete, thoroughly equipped for every good work*" (2 Timothy 3:15-17 NKJV).

11. Sin is real and Christians are given specific instructions detailing what actions are sinful. Christians are instructed to avoid sin and we don't have to do this alone. The Ten Commandments and the Sermon on the Mount are a good beginning. Read Galatians and Ephesians as well.

12. If, as Christians, we do become entangled in a sin then we need to repent, ask for forgiveness, and God will forgive our sin. God will forgive those who repent of their sins.

Now you have the complete non-negotiable Christian doctrine. With these 12 points anyone can receive eternal life and avoid the problem of being pushed around with every wind of doctrine.

Remember the last chapter "Flaws" and the real diamond. If you question a doctrine then hold it up to the light of Jesus and see how it looks. Does it hold true with the character of Jesus, and is it in conflict with any of these 12 points?

IS IT A DOCTRINE OR IS IT A TRADITION?

Some ideas that are presented as doctrine may not be founded in scripture and may be a tradition made up by a group of people with a certain point of view. The following two accounts may serve as illustrations to prevent an uprising over what I just said.

When I was a young guy, the teaching of the day in my Church circle targeted a certain denomination that could not be Christians. I was taught that they were not saved because they smoked. It wasn't until a number of years later that I actually met some from this denomination and became friends with some of them, that I found out that this was not an accurate assessment. While puffing on his pipe my new friend told me about how God was at work in his life—yellow teeth and all! Now go figure!

In later years it turns out that many of them no longer smoked. It wasn't that they came to believe that it was doctrinally wrong, but they just figured it out that it was dumb. Made them smell bad. Now that they have stopped smoking I guess they are now Christians. That's sort of an extension of the little rhyme: "Don't dance, don't drink, don't smoke, don't chew—and don't go with guys that do." This may be good advice for your single daughter. It is not, however, based in scripture. It is a tradition that can be thought of as a doctrine.

A friend of mine remembers growing up in a small prairie town. His church taught, "A Christian shouldn't go to the town barber shop." The following account is in my friend's own words:

"There seemed to be three distinct communities living in our small town in southern Saskatchewan. The family I grew up in was among the "Christians." We all attended a Church with a strong Bible-centered message, embracing a rich "grace" doctrine. There was a second group who attended one of several "so-called" Christian Churches in town, but whom we knew could not really be Christians because they smoked and drank, went to dances, used real wine in their communion (not the Welch's grape juice that we used) and sometimes could be found working in the fields on the Lord's Day—especially during the brief harvest time. Occasionally, a few of them were rumored to frequent the town's pool hall. Finally, there were the real heathen who seldom if ever attended a Church of any kind, smoked, drank, chewed tobacco, didn't hesitate to add a few cuss words to make their conversations more colorful, played pool and, we were sure, gambled on their games as well!

"That set us up for a problem. The pool hall was actually a room in the back of the town's bowling alley. We were expected to be Christ's representatives on Earth, and it was clear that Jesus would never have played pool, and as a consequence, because of its close proximity to the pool room, we were not permitted to venture into the bowling alley. A further, somewhat curious situation also existed due to the fact that another room at the front window of the bowling alley was home to the town's only barbershop. I was one of the lucky ones—my mother was an expert with a pair of scissors and a clipper—but many of the kids (and even some of the adults) who attended the only "Christian" Church in town typically had hair that looked as though the barber simply trimmed it around the bottom of a bowl that had been placed on their heads."

SOME DOCTRINE IS HARD TO UNDERSTAND BUT OUR SALVATION DOES NOT DEPEND ON IT.

In my simple mind I have found that this is the best answer I can come up with. God has chosen to not reveal some things to me. If I had the answer for every question then I would no longer have the need to trust in God. This drives me nuts, because I like to be in the know. Ask my wife and kids.

If you have ever traveled with a guide then you will understand this illustration. On a hunting trip to northern B.C. we were flying into a remote area with no airport, with a "bush pilot." The pilot picked a patch of beach on the river and headed for it. A bumpy landing but all was good. We then travelled on horseback for a day to an even more remote area. We were going to spend 10 days in the wilderness in total isolation from the outside world. Awesome experience!

The reason we had hired the guide was because we didn't know anything about the terrain or the conditions that we were going to be traveling. We were confident, however, that our guide did have the knowledge to keep us safe and prevent us from getting lost. Others that we know had previously traveled with this guide and all had gone well. Checking references is a good idea.

As it turned out, we had chosen the right guide, had a great trip, and returned home safely. The proof of the success of this illustration is that I have the pictures to prove it, and I am here to give you this illustration. No injuries and no fatalities. Great trip!

After 10 days of hunting and camping with our guide I had more knowledge about the area than on the first day. At the end of our trip, I did not have all the knowledge that our guide possessed. To gain that would take a lifetime, and then I too could be a guide. I am not the guide, so until I have all the knowledge I must conclude that I do not have all the answers and must follow. Sometimes I must admit this fact. **I DON'T KNOW BUT I AM LEARNING.**

In life, Jesus is my guide and he has what it takes to get me safely through this life. I do not understand everything that is in the "mind of God," but I am learning. This will take a lifetime and will not be complete until I see him face to face.

So why do we get into trouble with the stupid issues we create with the troubling doctrines that come across our path? I think the answer is very simple. I love simple answers. Many of the wise and religious folks that we look up to have not learned to keep it simple.

I DON'T KNOW BUT I AM LEARNING. Do you have any idea how difficult it is to utter those words? Trust me, I know! The hardest words for me to utter is, "I do not know." So now you know as well.

Let's look at a couple of examples that you may have run across. This one is huge. You must come up with the answer to move forward. To listen to some people, you would think the salvation of an unsaved world depends on the answer.

Post-Trib & Pre-Trib doctrine. I like to refer to this as the baby boomer doctrine. Another term is End Times. You hear this a lot around the RV Parks. If you don't think so, try this experiment: next time you are talking to a non-senior ask them for a rundown on the two doctrines. Hey seniors, it is great to talk and interact with non-seniors. Helps you maintain your center of gravity. You ask the question to a young person. You get that glazed over deer-in-the-headlights stare. Now shuffle out of your RV and open the same discussion with a senior. Pour yourself a coffee. You will be in the chair for a while.

News Flash! Neither of these terms are in scripture. Both viewpoints, however, are validated without a doubt by scripture, according to their supporters. They have been the fuel for many debates over the years and have caused more than one Exit. How dumb is that?

Want to join the debate? Since this doctrine is not in scripture I think we need the definitions to get started. The book of Revelation, however, does have part of this doctrine detailed. Jesus is coming back to Earth some day to gather up his children and then the Earth is going up in smoke.

Now before you set your hair on fire, we do know from scripture that Jesus is coming back to Earth. There will be a lot of power and fire and we better be watchful and ready. There are many Bible passages that tell us that Jesus will return. I know without a doubt that Jesus is returning and that the Earth will end. Jesus said it will be and so it will. See John 14:1-2. If it were not so then Jesus would have told us.

> *"Behold, I am coming quickly! Blessed is he who keeps the words of the prophecy of this book"* (Revelation 22:7 NKJV).

> 24 *"But in those days, after that tribulation, the sun will be darkened, and the moon will not give its light;* 25 *the stars of heaven will fall, and the powers in the heavens will be shaken.* 26 *Then they will see the Son of Man coming in the clouds with great power and glory. And then He will send His angels, and gather together His elect from the four winds,*

> *from the farthest part of earth to the farthest part of heaven"* (Mark 13:24-27 NKJV).

Post-tribulation rapture: This doctrine holds that there is a resurrection-rapture of living believers in Jesus Christ at the end of the age (or the "End time"). Post-Tribulationists believe that Christians will remain on the Earth through the three-and-a-half-year Great Tribulation period. This period starts at the Abomination of Desolation and ends at the Rapture. They will be gathered by the angels to meet Christ in the air (raptured) at Christ's second coming immediately after the Great Tribulation, and just before the Battle of Armageddon—and then return with Him as Christ descends to the Earth, to usher in the Millennium (World to Come) on earth.

Pre-tribulation rapture: (This point of view was not in vogue until after year 1830.) In the Pre-Tribulation view, a group of unfortunate people will be left behind on earth after another fortunate group literally leaves this planet—just before the rise of the Antichrist and the beginning of the Great Tribulation. Pre-Tribbers believe that the Wrath of God (rather than being a brief period following the Great Tribulation), refers to the entire Tribulation period—and since the Bible says that Christians are "not appointed to wrath" (1 Thessalonians 5:9), they believe that the saved will therefore be taken away to heaven just before the Tribulation starts.

The Bible doctrine of "being raptured" comes from the phrase "to meet the Lord in the air." *Rapture* is now the most common term, especially among fundamentalist Christians and in the United States. (I guess if you live in Europe or Australia you may have some problems with this.) The other, older use of the term "Rapture" is simply a synonym for the final resurrection generally, without a belief that a group of people is left behind on Earth for an extended Tribulation period after the events of 1 Thessalonians 4:17. This distinction is important as some types of Christianity never refer to "the Rapture" in religious education, but might use the older and more general sense of the word "rapture" in referring to what happens during the final resurrection.

So now you have it in a crystal clear version. No confusion and without a doubt correct and substantiated by scripture. Can I refill your coffee for you? It must be getting cold by now?

What do I believe? Sometimes I must admit this fact. **I DON'T KNOW BUT I AM LEARNING.** But my pressing concern is: what can I do today as a testimony to those in need? Jesus is coming back some day. Right! But it may not be until after I die however. So what about today?

Some great theologians have debated both points of view for a few hundred years now. Or at least since 1830. Both points of view are established doctrine. Both sides can't be right as there can only one truth in anything. My conclusion is that there isn't an obvious answer. I don't know. If it mattered so much, God would have made it clear.

My point of view then is based on Matthew 24:44 (NKJV): "*Therefore you also be ready, for the Son of Man is coming at an hour you do not expect.*" Have you considered that your meeting could be today, even if the rapture does not happen today? Also, remember that Jesus said in one parable, *"Occupy till I come"* (Luke 19:13 KJV). In other words, keep busy for the kingdom until he returns.

Death is often unplanned. Unless you are on death row the precise time of your death is not known. So what testimony to an unsaved world will you present today? How do you plan to be light to the world today? Who will you reach out to help today?

A meeting can take place in one of two ways.

1. You die and go to meet Jesus.
2. You don't die and Jesus returns and you are caught up to meet him in the air.

Either way you are going to meet Jesus—either by death or by rapture. Depending on your age, it is almost certain that it will be by death. All the debates in the world will not change God's plan for your appointment. Are you prepared? What is your testimony to the unsaved and those who are cold towards Jesus?

I have full agreement to the fact that there is a coming end to this world. It will go up in smoke, and Jesus will be returning as he said he will. I believe that the words of Jesus are true. I just don't know when. And neither do you, though you may be convinced that you do. So what is the answer?

Sometimes I must admit this fact. **I DON'T KNOW BUT I AM LEARNING.**

Wake up call! Look at today and make a difference as a Christian in an unsaved world.

> *"The days of our lives are seventy years; and if by reason of strength they are eighty years, yet their boast is only labor and sorrow; for it is soon cut off, and we fly away"* (Psalm 90:10 NKJV).

It appears that Psalm 90 could be accurate. According to statistics Canada in 2012 the average life expectancy for Canadian males is 79 and for females is 83. Here is the good news: I live in B.C. and B.C. has the highest life expectancy in Canada with males at 80 and females at 84. In view of these comments perhaps I should focus on being a light to the world for the possible 80 years I have on earth and not get embroiled in debates over the next thousand years. How much sand is left in your personal hour glass? What are you going to do for Christ today? Don't get distracted over doctrine.

One question for all, the young and the old: how much sand is left in your hour glass?

Time to bare my soul.

HEALING: I must admit that this is a huge challenge for me. I wrestle with this one Big Time! When health issues come along and a loved one dies then huge questions arise as to why. Me included. I have prayed for friends to be healed, and only a few short weeks later they die. I prayed for one certain individual to be healed from cancer. I knew without a doubt that if God healed him of this disease then the whole family would turn to Christ and be saved. He died. God sure missed that great opportunity.

I intend to come back to this in my own story of my personal Exit as the last chapter. Yes, I have decided to include part of my testimony. I have been waffling on whether I should or not. I made a decision. Just thought I would throw that in. We are getting close to the end, and I want to keep you going.

Now if the feeling of grief and failure isn't enough of a problem, I find Christians advising me that I didn't have enough faith—and they quote the scriptures about the promises of God to heal. Verses are quoted such as Mark 16:17-18 (NKJV): *"And these signs will follow those who believe: In My name they will cast out demons; they will speak with new tongues; they will take up serpents; and if they drink anything deadly, it will by no means hurt them; they will lay hands on the sick, and they will recover."* Pretty weighty scriptures.

This is not what I needed when my father-in-law had just died and I was told that it was my lack of faith and the problem was that we didn't take him to visit the right evangelist. The other reason he died is that I didn't pray the right prayer for healing.

Did you know that you can blow the whole promise if you pray the wrong prayer? That's some people's doctrine. But when your doctrine doesn't line up with reality then the answer is a process of "transference." Perhaps another term is denial. Transference is the art of shifting the blame for a prayer not being answered in a way people think it should have been, to the shoulders of the one praying. Shift the blame to the person that is praying and all is explained. Now we have an answer for the failure. Perhaps for the callous onlooker, but what about the person in pain from the so-called failed prayer?

People inflicting these distorted forms of doctrine on others fail to recognize that scripture is full of promises. Try this one for example: Hebrews 9:27 (NKJV) says, *"And as it is appointed for men to die once, but after this the judgment."* Yes, this too is a promise of scripture. We know that every person has an appointment to meet God some day. It most likely will not be by the rapture, so it will most likely be by death. Hard to accept? We must learn to deal with this fact. If this promise was not true, then nobody would die. Wow! Population explosion big time!

All this talk of dying is getting heavy. Lighten up here. This is positive stuff! Deep breathing exercises.

We are confronted each day with many distortions of scripture and many doctrines that may or may not be correct. In many cases, I think some of them may only be partially correct as seen through a particular lens on a perfect day. True doctrine, however, will stand up no matter what lens you are looking through, and what day you are looking. Many doctrines have as their foundation a particular bias based on a distortion of scripture. See the chapter again on diamonds and flaws. When you are considering a doctrine, look at it for yourself in the light of your own scripture-reading and in the light of Jesus. Try more Bible reading and less book reading to study doctrine. Don't use the filter of others but the filter of scripture. God does speak through his Word. Try it!

Distortions can blaze a wide trail. Pick one. You will find distortions that will fit any of our daily needs. Doctrine is for sure important. This is the foundation of what makes us a Christian. Just study scripture to clean your filter.

Tip! Examine those who are presenting a doctrine from a potentially selfish motive. Yes, some that teach doctrine may have a selfish motive.

> 15 *"Some indeed preach Christ even from envy and strife, and some also from good will:* 16 *The former preach Christ from selfish ambition, not sincerely, supposing to add affliction to my chains;* 17 *but the latter out of love, knowing that I am appointed for the defense of the gospel.* 18 *What then? Only that in every way, whether in pretense or in truth, Christ is preached; and in this I rejoice, yes, and will rejoice"* (Philippians 1:15-18 NKJV).

We are presented doctrines on finances, health, romance, direction for your life. I am sure you can add to this list. It is long. The Bible is flawless. Be cautious to examine doctrines in the light of scripture before you plan your Exit. See how a particular doctrine lines up with the complete scripture. Examine the motives of the one that is teaching you this doctrine. Do they have something to gain if you follow their doctrine?

Sometimes I must admit this fact. **I DON'T KNOW BUT I AM LEARNING.** So keep learning until you meet Jesus.

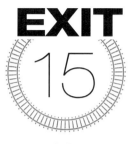

EXIT 15

MY PERSONAL EXIT

THE QUESTION HAS BEEN ASKED, "HOW ARE YOU RESEARCHING THIS topic and how long have you been working on your research?" It became obvious that without this chapter the book may not have any meaning. It would be a collection of a lot of theories. It became clear that I needed to introduce the experiment. My answer to the question is: "I have lived every chapter. It is one thing to research a lot of data to create theories, but having lived the data gives fuller meaning." I am the lab guinea pig.

For a few weeks now two key scriptures have been stuck in my mind. After reading this closing chapter perhaps they will stick in your mind as well. They have more importance than I previously thought, even though I have read them many times.

> 5 *"You shall love the LORD your God with all your heart, with*
> *all your soul, and with all your strength.* 6 *And these words*
> *which I command you today shall be in your heart.* 7 *You shall*
> *teach them diligently to your children, and shall talk of them*
> *when you sit in your house, when you walk by the way, when*
> *you lie down, and when you rise up.* 8 *You shall bind them*
> *as a sign on your hand, and they shall be as frontlets between*

your eyes. [9] *You shall write them on the doorposts of your house and on your gates"* (Deuteronomy 6:5-9 NKJV).

[1] *"Give ear, O my people, to my law; incline your ears to the words of my mouth.* [2] *I will open my mouth in a parable; I will utter dark sayings of old,* [3] *which we have heard and known, and our fathers have told us.* [4] *We will not hide them from their children, telling to the generation to come the praises of the LORD, and His strength and His wonderful works that He has done.* [5] *For He established a testimony in Jacob, and appointed a law in Israel, which He commanded our fathers, that they should make them known to their children;* [6] *that the generation to come might know them, the children who would be born, that they may arise and declare them to their children,* [7] *that they may set their hope in God, and not forget the works of God, But keep His commandments;* [8] *and may not be like their fathers, a stubborn and rebellious generation, a generation that did not set its heart aright, And whose spirit was not faithful to God"* (Psalm 78:1-8 NKJV).

Knowing your heritage and the faithfulness of God has great value. There is strength received from looking back to the times of God's faithfulness in my heritage. I realize that the things I do will become part of the heritage for the future of my family. The words contained in the passage of Psalms—*"You shall bind them as a sign on your hand, and they shall be as frontlets between your eyes"* (Deuteronomy 6:8 NKJV)—these words are true. Don't discount the value of these words.

If you are a new Christian and don't have a Christian heritage then this is your opportunity to create one. A legacy can begin with you. You can be the first in a long line to pass on the faithfulness of God to your future generations. Take this admonishment seriously. You can make a difference for generations to come. What legacy do you wish to create? The word "difference" is a two-edged sword. The decision is yours - Follow God - Don't follow God.

I am very fortunate to have a long heritage of a family that has chosen to depend on God. I am also privileged to have family members who have made it important to pass on these family stories of God's faithfulness. At our son's wedding I gave a speech as is customary at weddings—a father of the groom kind of thing. My topic was that it takes a village to raise a child. Each child's village is made up of family and friends who stand with you and your child as they are growing up. They pour into the child the values that your family holds true. I am fortunate to have come from a large village with a long heritage of trusting God. My children are reaping the benefits as well from the support of this village.

I come from an ordinary working man's family of four—my dad, James; my mom, June; my younger brother; Dean; and of course, myself. My mom was a stay-at-home mom. She did a great job of making our home a wonderful place to live. Our home was a hub of activity for me and my friends who were always welcome. I recall countless times that I would invite a gang of friends home to consume her fresh baking. Even to this day many recall the fun times we had at my home as kids.

My dad was a hard-working man who provided well for his family with a lifelong career as a postman with Canada Postal Service. He was not rich financially. Spiritually, he offered much more than the richest man could afford. He truly led our family by example and not just with big words. His walk with the Lord and leading his family was of greatest importance to him. Next to following the Lord daily, his family was his most important possession. Dad has since passed away but his legacy remains.

Participation in our Church was not an option. Mom likes to recall the fact that I was the first baby to be dedicated to the Lord when their Church moved into their new building. She has the pictures to prove it.

From an early age, attending Sunday School and Church was important. It was through the teaching of my parents and the Church that I found Jesus as my Savior one Sunday morning, April 7, 1957. I remember this day well. We celebrated with a special treat. My dad walked with me to the corner store across the street from the Church. He gave me five cents to spend on anything I wanted. I bought a red jawbreaker for two cents and dad said I could keep the change. My mom made sure that the event was properly recorded and it is still in our family history—including in the back of my Bible. Mom follows the teaching of Psalm 78 well. If anyone tells you that accepting Jesus at an early age is of little value… Not true! I remember it well.

As time progressed, I asked my parents if I could be water baptized. I was baptized on April 24, 1960 during the evening service. My aunt Viola phoned to tell me that she would not be able to attend the event. She and uncle Alex were at the hospital and she was soon to give birth to a baby boy. My cousin Arthur was born at the time of my baptism.

Once I was in my teens a great milestone was reached. I was now old enough to attend the youth group, "Teen Time." I had to be 13 years old to attend. At 15, I was eligible to be part of the youth council. I was very excited to become part of this group, the leadership group of the youth ministry. I later became the youth leader for the Church. This was back in the day when most ministries of the Church were by volunteers.

Church was not utopia, however. The good old days had the same warts as the Church of today. I recall various problems within the Church. It would start off with one group having an issue with the lack of good teaching. Another time, it was an alleged moral failure of a pastor. On another occasion a group banded together to follow a pastor to plant a new Church just down the road. Now we had two Churches with warts. I think I heard the term "Church Split." Enough of this talk. Things don't change when you add or subtract people.

Once school days were finished then came my high school graduation. Dad always stressed the importance of having a trade. Not working wasn't an option. I started working at gardening jobs around the neighborhood at 12. Starting at 15, I had a job on weekends and school vacations working at North Shore Shingle Mill on the maintenance crew.

This got me interested in steam engineering—not locomotives but generating electricity and heat by steam. I became friendly with the chief engineer of the mill and eventually got to work in the steam plant. He agreed to sponsor me in the required courses and record my hours worked towards my certification. Starting in grade 11, I took extra correspondence courses and a couple of night courses. This was before the days of online learning. That option would have been huge, but computers hadn't even been heard of. The extra courses helped to shorten the process once I was out of school.

Now graduation from high school was quickly approaching. I needed six months of full-time work on a high pressure boiler to finish my engineering training. I landed a job with Crown Zellerbach in Ocean Falls, B.C. This was a large pulp and paper mill and offered all the machinery that I needed to gain my practical training. This would get me my certificate as a Fourth Class Stationery Engineer.

Waiting wastes so much time! If I could graduate early and get out of high school I could speed up the process. As it turned out my grades were sufficient. I wasn't required to write final exams.

For work reasons, the school principle permitted me to leave on the first of June, 1966 and still receive my graduation diploma. I missed my grad day so the diploma was mailed to me. I bought a float plane ticket and headed for the north coast of B.C. This was pretty exciting stuff—my first time away from home and my first time on an airplane. A very small airplane. A Grumman Goose.

I don't think my parents were that excited about their kid who had never been away from home moving to some northern bush town to find his own place to live. In true motherly fashion, mom pulled out all the stops to find suitable accommodation. She located a Church in Ocean Falls. Actually, one of three Churches that existed there—Catholic, United, or Brethren. Brethren seemed to be the choice. Not the same as our Church, but it would do. Mom made a phone call to the Church pastor. Good news. A family in the Church was looking for a boarder. The agreement was made and I had fine accommodation living in the post office sharing a room with their 14-month-old son. A bit inconvenient, but it was in a Christian home. I was on my way.

This change in Church denomination created a new curiosity in my spirit. I joined the Wednesday night Bible study and asked for some materials that I could read to get up to speed. I had time on my hands after work. I had read the Bible cover to cover by the time I returned home in November. I also produced a few notebooks full of handwritten notes regarding the scriptures. I wanted to find out what similarities my new Church had to my Church back home. Both Churches thought they were different. I found they were very similar. We were all Christians.

A real bonus presented itself. Six Bible School students arrived in town to run the daily Vacation Bible School at the Church. Three girls and three guys. This created some great possibilities. The three guys didn't seem that interested in the girls, so I offered to help out for the summer.

Ocean Falls doesn't have any roads or automobiles as it is built on the edge of a mountain and follows the shore line of a large inlet. Sort of like living on the edge of a funnel that drops directly into the sea. It is nestled at the bottom of a high mountain at the end of a long fjord. One night in late August a family in the Church hosted a get-together for the DVBS group. The home was about a mile out of town on the Martin Valley trail. The walk out to the home went well on a nice sunny evening. Not so for the return walk home.

Seven of us were walking together just before dark—the three girls and the three guys and me. When we came to the foot bridge there were five guys standing there drinking beer. This didn't look good. We decided to just ignore them as much as possible, keep in a tight group, and walk directly across without eye contact. Sometimes this works with bears so perhaps drunks are the same?

The wheels fell off our plan. One of the drunks made some lewd remark and placed his hand on one of the girl's shoulders. I made some comment, not exactly sure what. For the sake of the readers, it is best I don't recall. I sort of zoned out, my brain shut down and the adrenalin kicked in. The three guys and the three girls in our party took this opportunity to run. They were more passive than me, I guess. I was left on the bridge alone with the five guys. Not good odds.

One of the drunks threw a bottle at our fleeing group and nailed a girl in the back of the head. Lots of blood. Our group kept running. Now the action started. Fortunately for me, drunks don't react quickly. I delayed the drunks long enough to allow my friends to gain some distance. Now my time to run. My injuries were minor. Good to go!

Once in town we went straight to the police station on the edge of town to report the incident. The injured girl went to the first aid post for stitches and the police asked us if we could identify the drunks. I answered, "When they come back into town I am sure I could." One thing about Ocean Falls: everyone coming back into town has to pass the police station on the trail.

The three guys of our group didn't want to get involved and they left with the girls. I sat on the porch with the RCMP officer and waited. Sure enough, about 45 minutes later here come the drunks. I managed to identify two of them—the one with a tooth missing and one with a bent nose. The others claimed they didn't know what happened and they didn't want to talk.

I assisted the officer in making the arrests and the two drunks were locked up for the night and the others were released. The next morning charges were laid and the two (Toothless and Bent Nose) were shipped out of town on the next plane for Vancouver. Police business moved swiftly in the North in those days. The bonus round: I was offered a job with the RCMP working on the weekends when I wasn't on shift at the mill. The pay from RCMP duty was enough to cover my room and board, so everything I earned at the mill could be banked. The real bonus, however, is the fact that God for sure did take care of us that night. What could have turned out real ugly resulted in me receiving some minor injuries. The head injury on the girl needed only a couple of stitches. No big problem other than a bad hair day for a couple weeks.

The rest of the summer went without incident and I returned home in October. By this time I had finished my training and on December 12, 1966 I received my engineer's certificate. First step of my goal completed.

Once back home I reconnected with my home Church. In the late 60s we saw a move of God in our Church. We had a youth evangelist visit for special meetings. The youth group was mobilized to reach out to the unsaved. A new problem emerged—a problem in the eyes of the Church leaders, that is. A lot of undesirable types got saved and decided to come to our Church. I was the youth leader at the time, and I found myself involved in this tempest. I was part of the group that was out bringing these kids in from the community. Through similar events, other Churches in the city also experienced this same move of God. It became known as the Jesus People movement. We made some connections with some other denominations and sort of joined forces. This had some issues as well. The other Churches didn't believe the same as us.

Enough of a reaction was created that the attendance of the youth started to diminish. (I wonder why?) The Church leaders decided that the problem of declining attendance needed to be fixed. The problem appeared obvious: we had no paid staff for the youth. That problem was resolved and the first paid youth pastor joined our staff. He was a great guy and became a good friend.

I observed a real phenomenon regarding paid staff. When volunteers are doing the ministry, they are just treated as normal folk. The volunteer effort works well as everyone is in this thing together. When a paid person comes onto staff, the volunteer effort seems to shift. A paid staff member has a different status. Once a person is paid by the Church they immediately gain status by the title that is bestowed on them. The term "pastor" creates a sense of increased spiritual respect and the attachments of the normal folk are different. The volunteers now become the support group for the pastor.

Even a greater problem lurks in the wings. When a volunteer steps down, the backlash is much less than when a pastor is dismissed. A volunteer takes a break and remains in the Church as one of the normal people. Not so with pastors. Very seldom does a pastor get dismissed. They usually resign. Why is that? For reasons I don't know, the youth pastor moved on and this created some fallout with the youth group. Once again some unsettling times followed.

My landscape started to shift as I moved into the 1970s. My career choice by this time had changed from an engineer to a stock broker. Today the term would be an investment advisor. I wanted to learn about business and I felt the fast track would be to work in the stock market. I tend to look for fast tracks. This turned out to be a financially successful move for me.

Things on the Church front started to shift again. As in the previous Exit chapter the tide became restless and started to turn. Some were leaving and there were some staff issues of some sort. By this time the Church had increased its paid staff and now some of these were being moved out as well. This created a problem as people had become attached to a staff member. A move always affects more than just one person. This was no different. A Church storm was in the making.

Now the other piece of the perfect storm: I was engaged to be married to a young lady. No need to speculate here. Yes, she was a Christian. All I will say is that our engagement ended. With the emotional turmoil I was now experiencing on both my Church front and with the ending of our engagement, my sales started to slip. Sales is a very emotional business and to be on top of your game you need all eight cylinders firing. I was running on about five cylinders instead of the former eight and with not much enthusiasm to succeed.

The world economy was showing signs of weakening and the stock market was not producing very good returns. With all of this going on in my life I decided to take some time off and leave my career for a short break. To clear my head and heart I took a part-time job with my uncle at his moving and storage company.

I didn't want to stay around and wait for the Church fallout to take place. I had enough already happening in my life without another distraction. I started to look for another Church and perhaps get a clean start on Church life.

I went to an evangelistic tent meeting that was the start of a new Church plant. The evangelist was a pretty flamboyant type of guy. He could really get people worked up. For some reason, he came to talk to me after the meeting. He proceeded to butter me up about all that God had in store for me. He then went on to say, "God has told me that you are to give me your wallet to further his work." I don't know why he picked me to receive this revelation. I didn't bite. I thought it interesting that for God to work in my life the recipient of my money should be the evangelist. I must become an evangelist.

For some reason he must have thought that I carried cash. I wasn't about to give it to him. I told him that he would have to wait until God spoke to me. I left the meeting in disappointment.

A few weeks later I met some young adults. They invited me to come and check out their Church. I had heard of the two pastors and the meetings were showing a lot of growth. They were seeing a move of God in their Church. A great group of young adults. Pretty girls. A fantastic choir and excellent preaching and teaching. I left my Church that was now further into their issues. I started to attend my new Church.

A few months went by when the pastors started suggesting that I should consider the ministry as an option. A bit of flattery was laid on me as to why I should take this path. I trusted them by this time and said that I would give this some consideration. They told me to pray about it. I decided to take their advice and so I went on a two-week fast. I fasted and prayed and spent time reading scripture. I didn't have a full sense of peace over this direction, but I did tell them that I would take a greater role in the ministry of the Church for a period of time and see what the Lord would lead me into. It was suggested that I become their "Timothy" just as Paul and Silas had their Timothy. I would be their trainee and take some evangelistic trips with them. I agreed.

As I moved more into their inner circle I started to observe things from a different point of view. I was feeling unrest and seeing things I don't think they suspected I was seeing. They seemed to be careless without thinking that I was picking up on the unseen.

One of the pastors would go on missionary journeys to Haiti. On his return he would have sea containers full of merchandise and he would sell this through his contacts in Vancouver stores. He would go on the trip at the Church's expense and then pocket the proceeds of the sales. I found that he was a "silent" partner in a store. I questioned this, and I was told that this was all going "to the Lord's work." I guess?

One day, the two pastors had a planning meeting and I was invited to attend. I owned a rental home in Richmond, B.C. that I had bought when I was 19. I bought this home after my return from working in Ocean Falls. This was rented out to provide some income to pay the mortgage. They suggested that if I was serving riches then the Lord would not bless my ministry. They didn't come outright, but the suggestion was very strong that I should donate it to them if I was serious about ministry—not to the Church, but to them personally. Same as the previous evangelist. I would be blessed if the pastor received my house as a gift. Perhaps I should consider being a preacher. Now my antenna was up!

A few weeks later, we went on an Evangelistic Crusade to Edmonton, Alberta. I used to sing solos, sing in the choir, and also lead music for some services. In the day the term was a "song leader." Now it would be a "worship leader." My role was to be the song leader for the meetings, minister to those needing prayer, and look after collecting the offering. They would also give me instructions on how to take an offering, and would let me speak and take a few offerings. They had a daily radio program and I would be given instructions and teaching on public speaking and would speak a message on the radio program from time to time.

We are now off to Edmonton. I drove their car to Edmonton and they took the plane.

We had good attendance at the meetings. And the offerings were of substantial size. These guys could really take an offering! Even I felt guilty if I didn't give. My instructions were to prepare any checks and donations received in a Church envelope for the bank deposit. Any loose cash that was not in envelopes I was to separate and give directly to them. I was told that this cash would be used for the direct day-to-day expenses of the Crusade. Hmmm. They were paid on salary from the Church, the expenses were paid for by our Church, the offering would go to the Church as receipted, but what about the loose cash? I was getting some uneasy feelings. They must have thought I just fell off the turnip wagon. Now my antenna was up again!

The next morning the two preachers had a breakfast meeting with a few invited pastors from the surrounding area—a group of about 20 perhaps. The purpose was to plan for future evangelistic crusades at their home Churches. The selection process for the lucky candidates went something like this: "You have been selected to join us at this meeting this morning as the pastors of some of the leading Churches in this region. The Lord is planning on using you and your Church to influence your surrounding area and be part of the coming revival." The flattery seemed to be working. The meeting got these pastors pretty charged up and motivated. Now my antenna was up again!

After breakfast the meetings were one-on-one with the individual pastors throughout the day. In a skilful manner, the general direction of the personal discussions went something like this: "What is your current attendance, and what is your average monthly offering, and your annual budget?" The Churches with the sizeable attendance and the larger offerings were the chosen ones for the planned coming revival. Future meetings were scheduled at these Churches. This is my short form. They were much more spiritual-sounding in person.

Later in the day I asked the pastors why finances and attendance were criteria in the selection process as to which Churches we would attend. Their answer had a very spiritual spin on it. The Churches that were able to "sow the most seed" would be the first to be called to "the planting of God's crops." The Planter of the Seed parable was worked into this explanation. Now my antenna was up again. Of course! How could I have missed that fact?

Night time. I am in my hotel room. It is late. I am having trouble sleeping. I am wrestling with questions in my heart. The unseen things are troubling me. What may I be witnessing here in the name of the gospel?

One of the preachers has a room on the same floor as me. Down the hall to the right, across the hall, three doors down. It is about 2:00 a.m. I thought I heard a door click and the sound of whispering voices in the hall. I wonder? I crack the door open for a peek. Sure enough. A young lady dressed like a "working girl" is leaving his room.

I previously had had some niggling thoughts that something may be up by the way he reacted with ladies in the meetings. Even more surprising was the way ladies reacted to him. It is amazing. Put a suit on a guy and let him preach and some women think he is a rock star. But now this is more than a reaction in a meeting.

I wait until morning. My bag was all packed and loaded in the car. I confront the two preachers in the hotel restaurant. My words may have had some color. I told them that if I never see another preacher as long as I live it will be too soon. A few other words. I also made a vow to them that I would never so long as I live ever be part of a Church again and all of the fake swindling that takes place under the name of the gospel. I told them that their car would be dropped off at the Church and the keys in the mail box. Don't ever expect to see me or hear from me again. I am gone!

Anger! My anger was sufficient to reignite the passion that I had lost over the previous months' events. My home Church problems, my engagement, my career and…now *this*! Why? I had 14 hours to drive from Edmonton to Vancouver and plenty of time to stew about what I had witnessed. On the way home I was driving into a dark place. Anger was all I felt.

During this time I hatched a plan. Preachers and Church were fake and I wanted nothing more to do with this stuff. I knew very well what my personal attributes were. I couldn't use my attributes within the Church. I was no longer considering the possibilities of becoming active in some form of ministry. This was not going to happen. I decided to pursue what I knew I was good at. I decided that business would be my choice and I was going to be wealthy. Presently I was broke, but that would change.

I was working part-time moving furniture with a good friend. It takes two guys to work on a furniture moving van. Bryant was my partner at work. The part-time work was rather slow at the time and we had gone on the government dole. We were on government Employment Insurance, out of work. We did a few things to make a few bucks. We were getting restless as we are both meant to be productive. Sitting idle was a drag.

We were in the bank cashing our unemployment checks and I said to Bryant, "We should go into business. Why don't we buy a truck and start our own moving company?"

Bryant thought I was nuts. He reminded me, "We are broke. That is why we are cashing our unemployment checks." I told him the bank had money. "Let's go and talk to the manager and get a loan for as much as we can. We can then take it from there." Bryant said, "Okay, but you do the talking." We agreed on the new business plans. A lot can take place while standing in a line-up at the bank.

We presented our well-thought-out business plan and a few minutes later we were in business. This was May 1, 1971—the day we got our phone number for our new business. We had nothing, but we had a loan and a phone number. Ready to go!

We worked together for a time and then Bryant wanted to go back to his trade as a carpenter. He accepted a position as a building inspector and I paid him for his share of the company. It was a friendly parting. We just had different paths to follow. The company grew. Sales were good and the company was making money. It attracted the interest of a company from Alberta that wanted to expand into B.C. They made a generous offer to buy the company from me in 1977. I thought of the next step. With this amount of cash I would have new opportunities—the option to move onto another fast track forward. I accepted the offer.

I was already investing in real estate prior to the sale of the company. The next obvious move was to move into real estate full-time. This I did and have remained in this field ever since. I was on top and doing well in business. I was achieving my goal to make money. Things were great! Not so great, however, when you lack an abundant and full life. I drove into a dark zone when I left Edmonton that morning to return the preachers' car. I was still stuck in this dark zone. Actually, the dark zone shifted to a zone of Cold and Bitter. Don't care about anyone, and for sure not Church.

The 1970s were not a good decade for me. I was making money but I felt as if I was running with no destination in mind. Bitterness and Cold were the flavors of the day. The best thing that God provided for me during this time was my wife, Cherril. I never expected that she would marry me.

We dated for a couple of years, and the first year for sure had some potholes. We never talked about marriage. I think she knew that this was not a good topic to open up with me. By experience she knew that any talk about any type of emotional commitment and I would be gone. Marriage was not a topic of discussion as it meant the involvement of emotions. I had none. Who needs emotions when you can be bitter?

Back to my friend, Bryant. One day at work he told me that I was stupid. Guy friends talk to each other like that. That's how you know you are good friends. He told me that I was like a blind man running. He told me, "You need to break out of this dumb pattern that you are following and find a good girl to marry and settle down. You know who that girl is. You have gone out with her for two years and she is the only girl you have dated for over a year now. You keep this up and she will be gone. You obviously love her but you are so stupid that you have not told her that." He was right.

I bought a ring. It is good to have a good Christian guy friend to say you are stupid. Wakes you up once in a while. I didn't want to lose Cherril.

The proposal wasn't exactly like you see in the movies. Slow motion, hair blowing in the breeze. Didn't happen like that. I asked Cherril to marry me and I gave her the ring. She looked at me with surprise and said "Are you joking? Is this real?" Not exactly the reaction I thought I would get. I got over it. So far so good, she hasn't said no yet.

In fairness, I should have at least talked about this a couple of times with her before the launch. I didn't want to go there because I was sure that she would blow me off. I should have discussed this with her dad. It is customary to ask the girl's dad if you can marry his daughter. I wasn't going there. I was sure that he would say I was nuts for even asking such a stupid question.

I have told my kids a few times, "A guy like me would be the last person on earth I would want you to marry. Don't bother bringing him around." You don't have to be a drunk, or a gambler who is living the wild party life to be the wrong fit as a husband. Those are only symptoms of a deeper problem. I had the full-blown disease, but without the visible symptoms. I could hide the symptoms pretty well. My friends and family thought that I was okay. I was not free to develop the symptoms. The only thing I can say is, "Praise God for my family legacy!"

These words are so true:

> *"You shall teach them diligently to your children, and shall talk of them when you sit in your house, when you walk by the way, when you lie down, and when you rise up. [8] You shall bind them as a sign on your hand, and they shall be as frontlets between your eyes. [9] You shall write them on the doorposts of your house and on your gates"* (Deuteronomy 6:7-9 NKJV).

When I was tempted to develop the outward symptoms of a sinner I just could not go there. How could I disgrace my family and be the bonehead that would be remembered as the guy that messed it all up? This would be my part of the legacy. Grant Holcombe, the guy who walked away from God because of Church and a few hypocritical preachers. His children and grandchildren are a mess and not walking with God. Grant showed them the way. The family dumb guy! He perfected the art of cold and bitter.

I knew I was a Christian that was not living for the Lord. I knew that I had temptations that could have lead me into a dangerous place. I was in a very difficult place. I could not go and enjoy my sin, and I could not enjoy my place with God. What good was this? I was not free to sin and I was not free to worship the Lord. Just stuck!

I was fully aware of the stories that were told to me by my mom and my Aunt Viola that went back as far as my great-grandmother accepting the Lord as her Savior in 1862—how she always carried a small bottle of oil in her apron. No doctors in the area when you were a homesteader in Saskatchewan. If anyone was sick or dying you went to see the woman with the oil and she would pray and you would be healed. Perhaps not all that doctrinally sound. She wasn't exactly an elder but she anointed people and prayed for them according to James 5:14. Look at this one recorded around 1875. She even prayed for the livestock.

"Quoted from her journal." When their livelihood depended on animals, it was a common occurrence to see her take her little bottle of oil and go out to the sick animal and anoint it, as it said in the Bible, and pray for it. The animal recovered.

Another account from around 1880. Her third eldest son was at death's door with appendicitis. "While fasting and praying with another dear sister I anointed him with oil and laid hold on God's eternal Word for complete deliverance of my boy. My dear child started to get well. He vomited it all up, that terrible thing. It just looked like blood and earth mixed. Praise God! From that time he grew stronger. He was full well inside of a week."

These words and many words like these are written on the doorposts of the house containing our family legacy. Was I going to allow the conduct of a few preachers cause me to be the guy in our legacy to mess this up?

Cherril and I got married on April 6, 1974. The next few years were a learning experience. That's the best way to describe it. When Cherril gets to heaven she will have a few extra diamonds in her crown. It must have been an interesting journey walking with the Blind Man Running.

We are going to have a baby! Now for a guy that had no emotions, this is a big one! I sort of felt like saying something dumb again. Like, "How did that happen, as I am never home?" So busy at work you know. That wouldn't have been good so I said something very deep like, "Wow?"

Now the questions were huge in my mind. What am I going to do about this? I have nine months to get my act together. No pressure. Got it covered. I need a plan. Joy - Fear - Panic - Excitement. Perhaps running in a circle for a while and things will work out. Church. A dad needs to take his kids to Church. What Church? We need to work this out.

We decided that I would attend Church again. Not just a fly-past as had become my custom. Show up once in a while so the family and friends will still think that all is good. Shake a few hands. Tell people how busy I am. This gives a good excuse. People serving the Lord can be too busy to attend Church. Business, you know. All is good. Now that I was going to be a dad I need to pick up my game. We started attending the Church that had been home since my birth. We got married there. Good place for a re-entry.

Things didn't seem to have changed much. We would go out for lunch and the faithful were still stuck on the topic of the sermon: "We need to get back to that old-style preaching." They didn't like the color of the preacher's tie. Big stuff, you know! The finances of the Church were always at the top of the list. What changes were needed with the Church staff. You know the drill, so no need to keep working the list.

Cherril tells me my assignment for the coming week: "Keep your days flexible and open. Keep your pager on. Due date is approaching. Be ready to drop everything when I page you. Got it?"

The pager goes off. Call right now! Cherril. Of course I was at an appointment and a deal was about to happen. Not today. I borrowed the phone and made the call. Told my clients my wife is in labor. Got to head home.

Cover the car seats with a blanket. If her water breaks we don't want to stain the upholstery. Great! Rush hour and we need to get through the tunnel from Delta to Richmond. We make it. No stains. We still have time. No matter what I did, it didn't seem to be what she wanted. Confusing!

May 31, 1979. I see the most amazing thing I have ever witnessed—the birth of my first baby. A son! The nurse hands me this little bundle and says, "Congratulations! You have a healthy baby boy."

Words that no one else could hear in that room sounded like they were on a loud speaker. They went like this: "This is God and you are my son. What are you going to do to teach your son about me? Men have failed you, but I haven't changed. I am still your God."

The prodigal son just became a father! The ice man fell apart. I had a decision to make. Do I teach him to be cold and bitter like me? I know better. I want him to be a man after God's heart and I had better do something about it. The climb back home began. I know what I need to do. My disappointment with Church and preachers is not going to mess up my son. Put this behind me and move forward. Time to man up!

A few weeks after Lance was born we dedicated him to the Lord. There were two dedications that day: one for a baby and a rededication of his dad. I had made a conscious decision to rededicate my life to the Lord and get my life back on track. All should be good now. Just pick up and get moving forward. This is what I was expecting. Wrong assumption!

Things were not improving and the Church was still experiencing some challenges. With the new baby, it was also getting more difficult to make the drive to Vancouver. We were living in Tsawwassen about forty five minutes from the church. Why stick it out? We decided that we would look for a Church closer to home. A number of people who had previously left our Church had ended up moving to a certain Church nearer to where we lived. I also knew a lot of people from previous days when I used to visit this Church. We moved and decided that this would be our new Church home. Easy place to start over and make some new friends and connect with some old friends.

We are now at 1980. If you know anything about 1980, you know about the world recession that struck every living being at that time. I was not left out of the experience. Real estate was booming and I was in some great projects. My, how fast things can change! Two of my projects got stalled. Within a matter of a few weeks the economy went from great to disaster. The bottom fell out of the market! Big time!

I was in a business partnership with three other associates. They all had money at the start of the projects, so no problem. In order to get the financing required to complete these projects the banks wanted cross guarantees. The loan was not that big when I considered that only a quarter of it was my debt.

I learned about cross guarantees the hard way. When one person fails then the others are to pay off the debt of the one who defaults. One default would not have been so bad, but all three of my partners went broke. One left town to never be seen again. One got divorced and declared bankruptcy. The third also went broke. I was the last man standing. I was also broke.

I talked to God and started negotiations with him: "This is not supposed to be happening. Don't you remember that I have come back to you? This isn't going like I think it should. Dedicate my life to you and now this." I had more than one conversation with Cherril: "This sure went well! I come back to God and now we are broke. You don't even have cash for food and the business is in the tank. I am a wreck. Good plan!"

The dreaded day came. I was expecting the call. The bank called and wanted a meeting. I was to be at the top floor of the Bank of Nova Scotia tower to meet with the B.C. Regional Vice President. This didn't sound good. Can we reschedule for about 10 years?

I didn't want to go bankrupt but it looked like I might not have a choice. I was in debt for $1,200,000. Interest rates had now climbed to 23.5 percent. I was on the hook for the whole amount. My interest payments were now at $23,500 per month. ***Yes, per month!*** Not a typo. But I had no money, I had lost everything.

Another negotiation with God. We need a plan here. I was prepared for the meeting in advance. I felt that God would somehow help me through this mess. Not a common thought for me in that day. I made the bank a proposal and presented a business plan to prevent the need for me to go bankrupt and also to return the bank the return of their capital. I would take my losses but the bank would receive all of their loan back.

Short story: the plan in part would require that the interest charges cease, and they would lend me $150,000 to execute my plan. I had nothing, I owed them $1,200,000 and I was asking for a loan of another $150,000. How could they say no? I agreed to take nothing from the deal. Everything would go to the bank and I would take nothing. They were to call off their dogs in suits and give me some space. Dogs in suits, by the way, were their lawyers. Sorry, lawyers. These lawyers had big teeth. Not just one lawyer but three lawyers!

My proposal had a deadline for acceptance by the bank. Call me by noon the following day, or they would hear from my lawyer and I would file the papers for bankruptcy. I would then be free of my problem and it would be fully their problem. I had nothing more to lose as I had already lost it all. The meeting ended and I headed for the elevator. I was never so glad to exit a meeting. Trying to remain cool and calm in that meeting was the most stressful thing I have done. When under attack never show fear!

Talk about great timing! You will think this is a fabricated story. Unfortunately, it is so true. I just stepped off the elevator and into the lobby of the bank tower. My pager goes off and I am asked to call the pastor of my new Church. He wants to know if I can meet him for lunch. We set a time for 1:00 p.m. at his favorite restaurant in Burnaby.

My mind is racing. How could he know what had just taken place? Not one other person other than my wife, the lawyer, and my bankers knew what I was going through. Not even my parents. The pressure of people asking how things were going wasn't to be an option. Me and God are going to work this challenge out. How could the pastor have found out?

We sit down to lunch and he says the customary prayer. A little chit-chat and then he tells me what is on his mind. It is his role to stay in contact with the influential people of the Church. He considers me one of the leaders of the Church. News flash, pastor! I just started attending here about six months ago. "Beware of a flattering tongue," comes to mind. "This will cost me."

He has a great opportunity for the ministry of the Church. He has a contract with CBC Television to broadcast a gospel program Canada-wide. He wants to offer me the opportunity to be part of this great mission field. He only needs $50,000 to make it happen. Can he count on my help?

For sure he had no idea what meeting I had just come from! No worry there that anyone had found out my secret battle. In fact, it was clear that he didn't even care what I was going through. In fact, he didn't even ask first. I told him that I would need to pray about this and I would get back to him. If you want to slide off a difficult situation, pull the prayer card. Almost forgot: I got to pay for lunch. Not a problem. What is a bit more debt on my credit card at this time?

When I got home I unloaded on my poor wife. She is the right gal for me. She got me to settle down and think about what I was saying. She said something deep and compassionate like, "Just shut up a sit down for minute." I am not sure exactly what she said but it worked. We had a brief prayer together. She prayed. I listened.

Next day, just before noon. The phone rings and it is the Bank of Nova Scotia. My heart almost failed until I heard the words. The bank would like to work with my plan but it needed some adjustments. They were not prepared to lend me the extra amount that I had requested. My reply was that without this extra loan, I had nothing to implement the plan. "Who should I send the bankruptcy documents to? The next call after this call will be to the bankruptcy trustee." The banked caved in. The guy already $1,200,000 in debt and broke was granted another loan of $150,000 to start the fight back to sea level for the bank.

Cherril was quick to remind me that if I would just settle down and trust God we would be okay. Smart wife! But a broke wife looking after an 18-month-old baby. Married to a broke guy who couldn't buy groceries.

I took a long ride on my horse and had a conversation with God. My horse must have thought her rider was nuts talking to himself. Come to think of it, my horse had a great name for this time of my life. Her name was Lucky. Over the next couple of years I took a lot of long rides. First comment was to thank God for giving me the plan and for causing the bank to accept the plan. Second comment was the reminder that we were partners, God and me, and I am looking for his guidance to get our family through this challenge. Third comment was the agreement that if successful I would trust him and not get sidetracked by the future challenges that come from watching men and not relying on him. We made an agreement that day and it was time to go to work.

Short story for a change: it took about two years for God and me to get things worked out. The bank received all of the money back. I didn't go bankrupt. Minor problem was that I was still broke. No cash, just pocket money. The amazing part is that the pocket always had just enough to get us by. Most people never suspected that anything was wrong.

Bonus round: one of the local credit unions was in a financial problem. They were being run by a trustee and working to deal with some bad land deals that they fell into by foreclosures. A real big mess of the day. I bet you never thought that a credit union could also be in financial trouble? One of the employees from the Bank of Nova Scotia was now working for the Credit union and the receiver. The former BNS employee asked me if I would be willing to initiate the same plan that had been successful for my mess. Would I do this for the credit union? The best words I could have heard: "We saw that you had a degree of integrity and honesty and a sense of knowing just what to do at the right time. Will you partner with us?"

I reminded them that I had no money. I had lost everything. That wasn't the issue to them. They just wanted my expertise. We signed a deal. Two years later the problem I took on was resolved. About a year into the process another company with similar problems was referred to me. We also entered into a partnership and their challenge was resolved in about a two-year period.

I have learned to trust in God. Within five years of my great crash God had restored me to a position that was better than before the crash. I was no longer broke. The best part of this whole story: I am no longer broke in my spirit.

I haven't told this story very often. I still find it difficult to mention. This is the first time in print. But I often say this as my short testimony. The best experience of my life was the time that God allowed me to lose almost everything. I am careful to always put in the word "almost." I know myself very well. I think my wife and kids know me even better than I know myself. Because of who I am, and the need to be in control, I could have easily lost everything. I needed God to give me a time-out long enough to teach me to settle down and let him lead. Still forget it from time to time and then he catches my attention for a reminder. Sit in the corner for awhile for a time out.

- ✓ I have now learned that when men fail you, just walk away from it. Leave it in God's hands. Men will fail you but God never will.
- ✓ Your prayers may not be answered exactly as you expect. His answer is better.
- ✓ I have a wife that has stayed true and a real support for a guy who may be a bit of a challenge.
- ✓ I have two great children who have started their own families with two great mates. They both married Christians and are following the Lord. They are part of my legacy.
- ✓ I have three exceptional grandchildren and one more on the way. My wife heard its heart beating yesterday.
- ✓ The grandchildren are walking with God. I can tell by the way they talk and look at things. Our seven-year-old granddaughter asked Nana (Grandma) if she could buy her a Children's Study Bible. I expect that with the support of our family—and, above all, their parents—that God will be the top drawer of their lives.
- ✓ I have a great heritage of a family who is walking with God. With only a few exceptions, I have a bunch of nephews

and nieces who are walking with God. I can truly relate to the few who are facing questions. God is working on them. Been there, done that!

- ✓ Many people have come to us with their own set of challenges. Cherril and I have been given an opportunity to help some of these with our first-hand experience. We sort of learned our lessons on the job.

I have a couple of close friends who have been reading as I am writing. They are greatly appreciated! The following comment needs to be addressed:

"Would it be possible to add a few lines in this chapter that summarize your current view of "the Church"? The Church and pastors (men) don't come off looking too good in your story. I know they did not do well. But somehow you have come through this all valuing Christ's Bride, the Church. Your heart is to encourage people to be right with God personally, but also to be right with His people, and to not exit…"

My reply to his question: "If I felt that pastors, ministry, and Church had no value then for sure I wouldn't waste time attempting this book." If reading this book leaves people with a feeling of disappointment with the Church then I have missed my objective. Even worse if it gives justification for even one to complete their Exit! Then I have failed. But I trust that you have seen my heart and my passion for the Church in these pages.

God has chosen men and women to be the body of Christ as his Church. The spotlight may have appeared to pause on the ministry in this last chapter especially, but let the spotlight pause on the whole body of Christ. Not everyone that attends Church is spotless. For sure not me. Proverbs 14:4 (NKJV) says, *"Where no oxen are, the trough is clean; but much increase comes by the strength of an ox."* This about sums it up.

I have livestock in the barn in the real world. Every morning I become aware of this fact. I have horses in the barn and the stall is not clean. You have people in the Church and the Church will have stuff happening. That is what people do. Lots of "stuff." When my horses leave stuff in the barn, I don't shoot the horses and exit for the city. Some of you may. I clean the stall.

The Church, the body of Christ, is a body designed by God specifically for this purpose. The full body has all that is required to become the healthy Bride of Jesus to produce much increase. Every part has a function. From ears to hear the unspoken, fists to defend the weak, to eyes to see the unseen. When the body of Christ is not functioning according to God's design then I am disappointed. Perhaps that is what may be seen. I don't want the Church to fade away. I just want to hand out some scoop shovels and pitch forks and clean a few stalls.

True story: A Church is a prime target for con men. They try to take advantage of the unwary. A con man worked his way into a Church I know and after gaining acceptance he started his devious plan. Even pastors of limited means can be taken advantage of. The elderly retired pastor whom I respected very much was taken advantage of. He was talked out of his limited retirement savings by a silver tongue. A huge return was offered. It didn't materialize, needless to say. I was fortunate to have been able to get most of my pastor's money returned. Sometimes your pastor may also need some protection.

I have many contacts with some very good and ethical people in ministry. Family members are missionaries and pastors. Don't read something into my writings that I am not saying. Help the Bride of Christ get ready for her Groom.

Well, this is only part of my testimony. After reading this, I must come to the conclusion that I must be one of God's challenging children. My story doesn't stop here. But for now the writing of it will. As they say in the movies: TO BE CONTINUED. Don't you just hate when that comes on the screen?

If you are struggling, I pray that what you have read will help you to not lose your focus. Do not EXIT. You are part of a legacy. You are part of a body if you have accepted God's saving grace. Keep it that way and create a positive legacy for you and your family.

If after reading this you realize that you are not part of the body of Christ then that can change. Accept Jesus as your Savior, and that will be the beginning of your change.

The publisher asked me if I can take one line or paragraph for this book to sum up the theme. Here is the quote:

The words that no one else could hear in that room sounded like they were on a loud speaker. They went like this:

"This is God and you are my son. What are you going to do to teach your son about me? Men have failed you, but I haven't changed. I am still your God."

> 6 *"I, the Lord, have called You in righteousness, and will hold Your hand; I will keep You and give You as a covenant to the people, as a light to the Gentiles,* 7 *to open blind eyes, to bring out prisoners from the prison, those who sit in darkness from the prison house.* 8 *I am the Lord, that is My name; and My glory I will not give to another, nor My praise to carved images"* (Isaiah 42:6-8 NKJV).

BE A BUILDER AND NOT A WRECKER

I watched them tearing a building down,
A gang of men in a busy town.
With a ho-heave-ho and lusty yell,
They swung a beam and a sidewall fell.
I asked the foreman, "Are these men skilled,
As the men you'd hire if you had to build?"
He gave me a laugh and said, "No indeed!
Just common labor is all I need.
I can easily wreck in a day or two
What builders have taken a year to do."
And I tho't to myself as I went my way,
Which of these two roles have I tried to play?
Am I a builder who works with care,
Measuring life by the rule and square?
Am I shaping my deeds by a well-made plan,
Patiently doing the best I can?
Or am I a wrecker who walks the town,
Content with the labor of tearing down?
– Unknown

ABOUT THE AUTHOR

GRANT HOLCOMBE WAS BORN IN VANCOUVER, B.C, CANADA. Gaining insight into the investment field as a stock broker and investment adviser he grew restless to own his own company. In his twenties he launched his first company which he later sold as a profitable business. Next he obtained his real estate license giving ample opportunity for growth. He is the owner of a Real Estate Agency and Construction company.

Grant frequently shares his knowledge and experiences by teaching real estate to realtors as part of the government post licensing program. Part of an active public speaking schedule means he is often invited to speak to both church and non-church groups on various topics. His many life experiences add color and humor to the chosen topic.

Grant was born into a Christian family and gave his life to the Lord at an early age. Committed to the local church he has served as a youth leader and Sunday school teacher. More recently he has served on church boards and committees including boards of charitable organizations.

Grant has experienced his share of church bumps and turns along the way. Some of these pot holes caused him to grow cold and disappointed with the church. From this viewpoint Grant has taken on the challenge of writing a book about the church. From firsthand experience he looks upon the church as an important part of a believer's walk and feels that the challenges are worth addressing. He walks the talk and is an active participant in his local church. Grant and Cherril attend Christian Life Assembly in Langley. His kids are active as well in their own churches.

Grant and his wife, Cherril, together are actively involved in assisting individuals and families needing help or counsel. Many with financial or emotional problems. From time to time they are specially blessed to be an "extended family" to those without a family and needing encouragement.

Grant and Cherril live in Langley B.C. and have two married children, three grandchildren, and one grandchild on the way. Grant enjoys activities on his small farm. His hobbies include hunting, fishing, boating, and bee-keeping.

For more information visit
www.exitsbook.com

Send feedback to
grant@exitsbook.com

Or look *Exits* up on Facebook.

Your comments are welcome!